VEDIC MANAGEMENT: THE DHARMIC AND YOGIC WAY

VEDIC MANAGEMENT: THE DHARMIC AND YOGIC WAY

KRISHAN SAIGAL

GYAN PUBLISHING HOUSE
NEW DELHI-110002

VEDIC MANAGEMENT
The Dharmic and Yogic Way

ISBN : 81-212-0719-3

Published in 2000 in India by
Gyan Publishing House,
5, Ansari Road, Darya Ganj
New Delhi-110 002

Phone: 3282060, 3261060 Fax: (011)-3285914
E-mail: gyanbook@del2.vsnl.net.in
Visit Our Web Site At http://www.gyanbooks.com

Laser Typesetting at A.S. Printers, Delhi

Printed at Mehra Offset Press, Delhi

CONTENTS

PREFACE

The conflict and tension between the negative and the affirmative approaches of the Vedic religious quest underlie the story of the conflict and tension between the 'orthodox' Vedism on the one side and the traditions of Buddhism and Jainism, which espouse with varying emphases 'homelessness' or ascetic withdrawal as the only spiritual option. Within Vedism itself, it is present in a discursively unresolved manner between the rival demands of understanding spirit as subjectivity and inwardness or alternatively, as holistic and integral. In a holistic view of spirit, what is without and what is within are valued alike. They are but the two sides of the same coin, so that no special significance is accorded to inwardness and interiority of life, except heuristically and there is no exaltation of the ascetic vocation.

This inherent tension between the inner and the outward and its harmonization through the processes of *dharma* and yoga, is what will be explored in this book. I begin with a delineation of the Vedic system. The Vedic seer, pure of mind and heart, embraces all aspects of human life or nature, harmonizing material-vital existence and physical-intellectual life. The uniquely Vedic concept of *yagya*, 'sacrificial rite', is to the seer the path to the knowledge of truth and everlasting happiness. These points of harmony are further brought out in *rita*, the universally unitary and obligatory principle which in turn leads to the realization of the unity of being, the cosmic and transcendent reality called the *purusha*. The Vedic sages discovered the *purusha* not only as immanent in the universe but also as the very core of the human self.

There is focus also on the spiritual import of *yagya*(s), the Vedic 'rite' par excellence. Through the sacrificial rite human beings play out their active and conscious participation in the gradual process of purification and upgrading. The sacrifice spans cosmic, vital and corporeal existence and brings about a 'second birth' which is described as the fountain-head of the flow toward the final goal of all the three modes of living—cosmic, vital, corporeal.

Vedic management, which is deeply imbued with a value system encouraging peace and concord in society, seeks to attain selflessness and cooperative behaviour through the 'sacrifice'—of the ego, of opinions, of strongly held beliefs. Stress of the Vedas is also on individual self-fulfilment which in its view optimizes the behaviour of the collective organization both in the social and the political spheres.

Thereafter I go on to consider the Upanishads. The Upanishads bequeath to spirituality a unique conception of spirit and spiritual knowledge and therefore, also of salvation. However, this does not mean that the later tradition, particularly the classical philosophical tradition of Hinduism, saw it with full clarity. Identity, which is the truth that resides at the centre of the Upanishadic approach to spiritual knowledge, is not a concept or an idea but 'a fullness that makes everything full.' Everything in the world as directed by the unseen logos—*vak* in the Vedic language—leads to that identity. Yet without the advantage of its light, it is not easy to see how things in the world, principles, relations, arrangement of concepts, inferences, and deductions, themselves unaidedly could lead to it. If the spiritual journey is from ignorance to knowledge, then it is logos that puts us on the way. Logos enacts the directional movement implicit in the posture called Upanishad.

The Upanishads interiorize the Vedic thought thereby developing the yogic way of meditation and contemplation. The attatinment of peace and serenity was to be through a process of purification and the attainment of knowledge through the harmonization of the rational and intuitive minds. The Upanishads enlarge on the Vedic system by stressing the need for liberating oneself from the stresses of life through work geared to the attaining of a serene contemplative and calm mind.

In Chapters 4 and 5 , I consider the concept of *dharmic* management as applied to social concerns and the polity. It needs to be noted that at that time these were the two that needed to be optimally managed. In the social sphere Vedic thought created a system in which the prime consideration was self-fulfilment of everyone through an enlargement of consciousness. In the polity the stress was on maintaining social cohesion and advance through the king being a *raja-rishi*, a seer-king who worked solely for the welfare of society.

Dharma is one of the most pervasive concepts of Vedic spirituality. As a social concept, it refers to the moral code, law, natural and positive and also, pre-eminently, to the various duties of individuals. The normative ordering called *dharma* in its legal, moral, social, and political aspects is the subject of exploration in the *dharma-shastra(s) and the arthashastra(s)*. The epics, namely the *Ramayana* and the *Mahabharata*, on the other hand, exemplify an understanding of the spirituality of *dharma* in concrete settings. The epic heroes are idealizations of character representing the different stations of life the *dharma* recognizes. Not only the seer and the recluse but also the ideal king, ideal wife, brother, friend, the diligent student, the citizen in his vocation are presented in these epics.

Social structure can be viewed as broadly political in the Western classical sense. The prescription of social order is a type of political thought outlining the best human order. In this context caste in the light of spiritual texts, is seen as a manifestation of a beginningless justice which is sovereign over all things. The *Ramayana* can be analyzed in terms of the filial and social roles of the chief characters: Rama is the ideal son, husband, king and friend; and Sita, the ideal wife. Bharata, even more than Rama himself exemplifies an ideal brother. *Dharma vis-a-vis* the mythical universe of gods and animals and forces of nature means cosmic harmony sustained through non-interference by all the inhabitants of the universe. *Dharma* is human *dharma*, a model to be emulated even by non-humans. The *Mahabharata* focuses on the spiritual teachings of the epic, extolling *dharma* as both *sakama*, 'with desire,' and *nishkama*, 'without desire'. It teaches non-violence yet does not consider war an evil. There is really no contradiction, since *dharma* is different from rules of morality and the two may or may not go together. *Dharma* and common morality represent a two-level ethics in which the latter is subordinate to the former and exception is given to the latter by this relation. One can distinguish between the *Ramayana* and the *Mahabharata*, by stating that while in the *Ramayana*, God himself had come to set an example of a life of *dharma* through mortal sufferings, in *Mahabharata* humans set an example.

In Chapter 6 we explore the system of yogic management as laid down by Sri Krishna in the *Bhagavad Gita*. Yoga is generally taken to be the art and science of reaching down inside oneself and summoning vital resources. It is similar to commando training, where the trainee tackles more and more difficult obstacles until he can cascade down cliffs. Yoga, however, is more than an overcoming of obstacles. The most pervasive feature of the discipline of yoga is a positive, spiritual pursuit imbued with a quest for freedom and immortal life, harnessing all the three built-in avenues which are open to human beings in their life of endeavour—body, speech, and mind. There are two areas of yogic disciplines: The body-behavioural yoga, that is, the yoga of human action—the yoga, in other words, of being-in-the-world represented in the teachings of the *Bhagavad Gita*; and the yoga of *Patanjali*, prima facie a psycho-mental discipline, though inclusive among other things also of physical cultural aspects.

The transformation of the mind, which is the central yoga of Patanjali, is considered not to be achieved through one's effort or practice but as the unifolding of nature's own potential tendency. Yoga merely eliminates the obstacles of the natural unfolding of oneself so that one may realize one's true spiritual nature. *Purusha* the 'spirit' simply is. It is independent of all the forces and controls 'nature'. In the *Bhagavad Gita* a more holistic yoga is taught in the *buddhiyoga* with its emphasis on integrated *buddhi*, 'intellect', which can culminate in a vision of the *purusha*. Identifying the different senses in its cosmic and individual connotations, the *Bhagavad Gita* finally focuses on *sthira-buddhi*, 'steadfastness of intellect,' which has a key role to play in controlling the mind. Truly speaking, in this yoga it is the self-transcendence of *buddhi* which leads to integration with ultimate reality. The contemporary relevance of this idea is the crucial distinction that it makes between transcendence and denial. This is crucial for modern life, for not only does it not deny the mind but also acts as a corrective to its hyperactive tendencies.

The yoga of the *Bhagavad Gita* makes management more of an art than a science; making it flexible and creative; leading to bliss and happiness. This it does by making the Vedic principles contextual to the situation and stressing on the need for making the mind calm and 'silent'. The aim of the yogic management of the *Bhagavad Gita* is to lead to harmony of the internal and external management of the organization thus, integrating managers with those whom they 'manage'.

The Vedic management system as elaborated in the Vedas and the Upanishads is a normative system while the Dharmashastras actualize a system based on the conditions prevalent in those times. The normative system enunciated by the Vedas and Upanishads is a decentralized system integrated by *rita* and *dharma*. The Dharmashastras developed systems of management based on Vedic thought and contextual to the simple systems of those days.

But management is not only theory but is also praxis. In this context it is not adequate to have a normative theory of Vedic management but also to examine whether it is capable of being practised in today's world. One person who did this is Gandhi in the earlier part of the twentieth century when he set up an organization in his struggle to free India from British rule. His success against one of the most powerful Empires known to history has been studied by me in Chapter 7 to understand the concepts, objectives and principles on which he organized the movement against British rule.

The normative Vedic management system has the following element:

- the management system is suffused with values.
- there is more stress on process (yoga and *dharma*) than structure.
- the system is non-hierarchical, a network and based on trusting the individual.
- accountability of top management is through the principle of stewardship.

I note how the Gandhian management system is based on Vedic values as well as the yogic system of the *Bhagavad Gita*. Gandhi made the whole system contextual to the twentieth century, making it a networking and flexible system thereby leading to the cessation of British rule by making the movement against the British a mass movement. The system was obviously very successful but the question that arises is whether Vedic management can succeed only in India or could also work elsewhere. I examine some post-modern management concepts in the concluding chapter of the book and leave it to the reader to take a view regarding the relevance of Vedic management principles in the post-modern world.

Krishan Saigal

1

INTRODUCTION

For the first time the people of the world have become one interlinked whole, with every one being affected by what happens to others. Science and technology and economic and political phenomena are increasingly imposing on us the obligation to treat the world as a single integrated unit. Currencies are linked, commerce is international, political fortunes are interdependent. And yet the sense that mankind must become one community is stilll a vague aspiration and not generally accepted as a conscious ideal or an urgent necessity moving us to common citizenship and the call of a common duty. Attempts to bring about human unity through institutional means and political adjustments, have proved abortive. It is not by these devices alone, that the unity of the human race can be accomplished. For this to occur there has to be some common ground, some understanding of other cultures and societies, some accommodation to the thoughts and views of others.

The European culture has been dominant for the last few centuries. Ever since the Renaissance, with the subsequent developments in science and European colonization of the world in the nineteenth century, the European ethos has been dominating. The only past known to the Europeans emerging from the Middle Ages was the Biblical and the Graeco-Roman. So these were the culltures studied and interpreted during the Renaissance. Now that we have the whole world for our cultural base, the process cannot be confined to the study of Isaiah and Paul, Socrates and Cicero. That would be a failure of perspective. For there are others also who have participated in the global human drama—the prophets of Egypt, the sages of China, the seers of India.

Of the living non-European civilizations, the chief are the Islamic, the East Asian (Chinese, Japanese, Korean, and so on) and the Vedic. The Islamic has the same historical background as Judaism and Christianity, and so is somewhat better known in the West than the Vedic and Chinese civilizations. The East Asian system, especially its Confucian and Buddhist aspects has also been studied in recent times, especially since the development of Japan and the tiger economies of the Pacific rim. But Vedic civilization has largely been left unstudied especially in so far its impacts on management are concerned.

Organizations and management systems have been there since the beginning of human society. Even when man was a food gatherer and cave dweller, he realized his fraitly, the dangers to which he was beset, the insecurity of life. But man could think. He could reason. He looked around him and drew lessons from nature. He watched animal-kind and drew lessons from their behaviour patterns. And cogent thinking and analysis led him to form groups, for he had realized that he could not do everything by himself. And groups needed to be managed while management needed organizations.

As man developed and matured, so did his individual and group behaviour. Civilization was the visible manifestation of progressive group behaviour. Great cities came up, economies flourished to the envy of others—wars were fought and civilizations were razed to the ground or burnt off the face of the earth. In their place sprang up new civilizations, better equipped, better trained and better organized and managed to face the hazards of life.

Each succeeding civilization tended to be more complex than what preceded it. Though management science is a fairly recent development, it is possible to argue that all human beings are practical social scientists striving to understand the world around them and work out guiding principles on which to base their behaviour. And, in a sense, all human beings are managers too; people struggling to cope, to manage, to shape their destinies. To survive in the world we have to manage our situation, to meet our material needs and to stay sane we struggle to exert some control over the environment around us.

As mentioned above, 'we have to manage'. This suggests that all humans are managers in some way. But some of them also take on the formal occupational work of being managers. They take on a role of shaping aspects of human social structure and culture in parts of our societies—those parts we call work organizations. But these managers are not supermen and women. They have all the human anxieties, inadequacies and needs for meaning to be found in those whom they are meant to 'manage'. Managers' work thus involves a double essential task: Managing others at the same time as managing themselves.

But the concept of management as it is practised today is that 'managers' are separate from the 'managed'. The consequence of this is that managers are pressured to be technical experts, devising rational and emotionally neutral systems and corporate structures to 'solve problems', 'make decisions', 'run the business'. These 'scientific' and rational-analytic practices give reassurance but can leave managers so distanced from the 'managed' that their capacity to control events is undermined. And they also tend to leave managers isolated from the essentially human community which the organization might be. This can mean that their own emotional and security needs are not handled, with the effect that they retreat into all kinds of defensive and ritualistic behaviour which undermines their effectiveness as people moulding and maintaining a 'healthily' and productively cooperative organization.

Moreover, management as we know it today is largely an American construct based on European roots. Historically modern management has developed as a discipline over the past couple of centuries. The first organizations of consequence in Europe and America, where the discipline of modern management developed, were governmental, religious and military institutions. From these came the initial concepts of leadership, the chain of command, coordination, control and functional specialization. The Roman Empire and the Catholic Church were particularly influential. Firstly, they experimented—not altogether successfully with decentralization, as this was an inescapable consequence of their great geographical dispersion. Secondly, in an effort to harness the centrifugal forces of decentralization, they established control systems that sought to impose uniform creeds of belief, norms of membership, and codes of behaviour. The Church had a major advantage: as Western culture's premier custodian of man's relationship to God, it commanded a special place in Western societies. It served their highest-order aspirations and thus could really support and lay claim to their loyalities.

By the sixteenth century, the Roman Empire was long gone but the Church remained—as a single, dominant organization in European societies. The scope of activities, however, simply outdistanced its capacity to sustain them when in that century and the next two, the meaning it provided dimmed because of the challenge posed by the growth of science and mercantilism. The ensuing turmoil permitted the gradual emergence of nation-states with governments capable of providing many social and military services. And, greatly affected the way organizations are viewed today.

In contrast to the Eastern societies of India, China or Japan where holistic views prevailed, Western society evolved separate institutions with separate spheres of influence: the Church emerged as the custodian of man's faith and spiritual life while governmental and then commercial institutions were given the role of providing for man's worldly existence. Not unexpectedly, Western political and organizational theory evoled to legitimize this duality as a natural state of affairs. Machiavelli, in the sixteenth century, was one of the first to consider management as a function separate from moral law by advancing an amoral theory for the organization of state practice.

The coming of the machine age was the next major event in shaping Western views of man, organization and society. The Industrial Revolution, with its stress on mass production, diminished the importance of the skilled trades and the social affiliations obtained through them. The emergence of the concept of 'factors of production' (land, labour and capital) had revolutionary implications for the Western view of humankind. Humans (the labour content) were no longer regarded as an inextricable part of the organic whole of society. Rather, the person, as labourer, became an objectified and standardized component of the production process. Not surprisingly, this view of "labour" tended to divorce man as a social and spiritual being from his "productive" role at work.

This separation of the ethical or spiritual element from the material was reinforced by the growth of value-free and so-called objective science. The Newtonian-Cartesian stress on reductionist and logical thought, and the publication of Darwin's theory of evolution and its stress on competition and the survival of the fittest, had major impacts on religious organizations which had their own cosmology and stressed on faith and co-operative behaviour. The tremendous importance and prestige of science gave a further fillip to the development of an objective, value-free science of management in which culturally derived values or ethical considerations had no role to play.

Industrialization in the nineteenth and twentieth centuries also fostered a great many large enterprises whose variegated and diverse activities made even more complex organization necessary. Max Weber's writings in this period stressed the desirability of the "bureaucratic institution." Weber espoused the view that the bureaucratic form was superior to all others—as indeed it was to the alternatives then available. One result of Weber's influence is that the factors he used to discuss organization—size, complexity, formalization and centralization—remain today the principal dimensions along which organizational designs are thought about.

The large corporation began to emerge as a dominant organization in Western society around the turn of this century. As the West tended to lead the rest of the world in spawning such enterprises, it is not suprising that the so-called modern management dealing with such large entities is largely a Western creation. The scope of activity of these large and diverse enterprises required tiers of management and delegation of authority. But how could those without ownership and a financial stake in the enterprise be trusted? Nearly half a century was needed for the concept of professional management to establish itself.

The question that had to be answered was as to how should these new "professionals" manage? The principal problems facing them were and are (1) how to organize efficiently and delegate responsibilities and (2) how to reward and motivate employees, as well as, how to control resources and ensure efficient and effective results. It needs to be noted, however, that the way in which any management solves these problems in a society is in itself a measure of the values that exist in that society. For management systems are in their essence culture-bound. And this is something lacking in Western institutions.

The reason is that Western institutions as a response to the problems faced, turned to organizational structure and formal systems to cope with these challenges. The result was that not much attention was paid to the social, spiritual and cultural parameters. As a result, the holistic vision of earlier institutions like the Church faded into oblivion.

Today, a large body of management literature has grown, mostly of American origin. In the literature, the mercantilist origin of management has been accentuated to the extent that today's management theories and systems deal largely with business enterprises. One result of this has been the development of very sophisticated tools of management based on rigorous analytical study in the context of the optimizing of financial returns. The flip side has been the relative neglect of public institutions whether of the governance, voluntary or not-for-profit type. Based on the earlier tendencies in the European civilization (the Church and the Roman Empire) of laying down uniform forms of behaviour, modern management theorists have also tended to regard their prescriptions as being universally applicable.

In such a milieu, the question that obviously arises is whether there is any need to study management based on Vedic civilization especially, as so many well established and time-tested management principles and tools are available? It seems that for a number of reasons such a study would be useful. This is attested to by the development of a new, and an eminently successful system of non-Western management, namely the Japanese one. Though the debate rages as whether there is any real difference between the Western and the Japanese systems, there is no doubt that the study of Japanese management has enabled American managers to gain fresh insights into new management concepts and ways of managing.

For example, Christopher[1], Feigenbaum and McCorduck[2], Fuse[3], Taylor[4] and Wolfe[5] have emphasized the Japanese interest in taking maximum advantage of the new "information age" by investing in the "human capital" of science graduates and engineers necessary to both create a new, independent Japanese "wave" of information technology and then by virtue of their heavy investment in this industry permit them to ride the crest of the wave they have created by becoming the world leaders in the development of this technology. The concept of human capital in the context of the formidable effort the Japanese are making to invest in this industry, marks one of the elements of Japanese management that most American authors on Japanese management (and indeed American authors writing on the state of the United States economy) agree is clearly transferable as a viable component of an overall industrial strategy these authors wish to see established in America. This has made human beings prime movers rather than mere objects of the process of management and thus moved them to centre stage. The fact that this stress on the human being flows from Buddhist culture shows the advantage of looking at management from other cultural perspectives.

The accent on acquisition of knowledge and thereby building up "human capital" is, as we shall see, the very essence of Vedic thought. The manner in which this can be done is spelt out in great detail in the Vedic scripturs with the stress being on the whole man. A study of management systems as they flow from Vedic thought would thus be a valuable contribution to the ongoing debate on how to effectively manage the ongoing Knowledge and Information Revolutions.

Also as Pascale and Pascale say when discussing Japanese management:

> ...managerial reality is not an absolute; rather, it is socially and culturally determined. Across all cultures and in all societies, human beings coming together to perform certain collective acts encounter common problems having to do with establishing direction, coordination, and motivation. Culture affects how these problems are perceived and how they are resolved. Societal learning also establishes horizons to perception.[6]

As globalization takes place and the problems of management whether in governance systems or in commercial undertakings have to be not only multi-national but also multi-cultural, the need to study other cultures arises. Besides, roots of human motivation lie in cultural values. So a study of diverse cultures and the management principles that flow therefrom is a necessary prerequisite for globalised management systems. Also as Drucker points out, management has always been polycentric and has to be tackled by men of many nationalities and races. According to Drucker:

> While management is a discipline—that is, an organized body of knowledge and as such applicable everywhere—

> it is also culture. It is not value-free science. Management is a social function and embedded in a culture—a society—a tradition of values, customs, and beliefs, and in governmental and political systems. Management and managers shape culture and society.[7]

Today as sustainable systems are seen to be very much in need of diversity to survive, there is merit in studying non-Western systems. The main such systems are the Vedic, the Buddhist and Islamic. While the concepts and value systems of the latter two are somewhat familier to the West, the Vedic system is largely unknown though concepts like yoga, transcendental meditation, non-violent non-cooperation have recently entered into Western discourse. The methodology of the Vedic system is also something the Western mind cannot easily grasp. Whereas Judaism, Christianity, Buddhism and Islam have a founder, the Vedas have none. Also there is no one book or scripture on which the system is based (and in this it is somewhat like Buddhism) unlike the three Semitic systems. Therefore, a study of the Vedic system could bring out some novel managerial insights.

There is, therefore, something to be learnt by studying the concepts of management that derive from various cultures and value systems.

Vedic Management

The Vedas are arguably the oldest surviving records of a continuing civilization. Dating from anywhere between 6500 BCE to 2000 BCE, they are an important part of the heritage of humanity. As Panikar points out, the Vedic lore is one of the most stupendous manifestations of the spirit. Its deepest function is best served, as of other religious and cultural values of mankind, by sharing it in a spirit of fellowship with humanity at large. This sharing, however, has to be a living communication that is free from any tinge of propagonda or proselytization and as a human experience that is "capable of enriching and challenging modern man in an age when, for better or for worse, he is inseparably linked with his fellows and can no longer live in isolation".[8] This lore, and the managerial system that evolves from it, could thus form a 'mirror' in which modern management science can see itself and thereafter evolve into a truly global, transcultural system.

There is great deal of truth in the fact that the external problems which torment man are really projections of the internal problems which he has failed to solve within his heart and mind. There is no adequate answer to the principal questions of how to manage—whether it is the realm of politics, society or economics—without first finding an adequate answer to the larger questions of life itself, which necessarily include the questions: "What is man?" and "What are the real objects for which an organized society exists." Unless we lay hold of correct answers to these questions, we shall only be working in the dark and wasting energies quite uselessly, or worse, gravely harm the human stuff out of which society is made.

The problems which press down on humanity are only apparently political, social or economic but their background remains moral and metaphysical. No solution can be a fundamental one if it ignores these two elements. There is no way in which humanity can save itself from the danger which confronts it if it leaves out the spiritual way; every other way if taken alone will yields only failure as its result in the end. Only when humanity has the sense to perceive this and the courage to admit it; only when it has the humility to declare that its management systems need spiritual values to become truly holistic will the highest powers of humanity be unleashed and appropriate solutions found. It is in this context that religous scriptures have a role to play. While it is not claimed that the Vedas have an exclusive role to play in this regard, it is suggested that they do suggest methods and a path which modern man could usefully employ.

The term 'Vedic', or the more commonly used word 'Hindu', refers to the spiritual life of the people of India or, more correctly, of Bharatavarsha, the 'world of Bharata'. The latter expression is not merely the geographical equivalent of India in vogue before the advent of the English term Hindu (which etymologically means the land of the

Indus River), but it signifies a single, though cumulatively diversified, cultural area like a pyramid inverted or, better, slanted on the side picturing its horizontal expansion. Vedism, which again was indigenously named to mean 'eternal religion' *(sanatana dharma)* or 'revealed religion' *(vaidika dharma)*, labels the spiritual quest of a people rooted in a single cultural soil. One may understand this feature by contrasting it with a case like Buddhism, which also was pre-eminently an Indian religion but was not determined by the circumstance of its rootedness into the culture of the area of its origin and unfolding. On the contrary, being essentially a homeless wisdom, a mendicant and missionary faith, it was a movement introduced in historical time into the society where it made itself at home and into a culture whose colouring it readily took.

Vedic spiritually, in contrast to the Buddhist, does not give attention only to 'worldlessness'. The Vedic concern and preoccupation was more with the order of the world–cosmic, social, and the individual—which it regarded as a given. The sacred order is not considered to be man-made but given in the nature of things. "The four-fold order was created by me" says the *Bhagavad Gita* (4.13). Likewise, the Vedic spiritual tradition sanctifies the life of the householder with his civic, social, and 'cosmic' obligations while, at the same time, providing a path to inward liberation for those wholly absorbed in the spiritual quest.

The Vedic spiritual journey is typically the affirmative way: Using things found in the realm of the 'many' as means to affirming the 'one'. The ascetic way of denial of the 'many' as a means for realizing the unaffirmable 'one' is also accepted but only for those rare individuals in which such a desire arises. "The day on which there is non-attachment (felt) renounce even on that very day."[9] For the very reason of its intrinsic importance the ascetic way is sanctioned only in the light of an express requirement or a felt call as a special vocation—it is not a prescription for everyone. The watchword here is 'eligibility' (*adhikara*) which various from person to person. But all are equal in a spiritual sense though unequal in the material physical context. What this implies may be stated thus: The essential equality of all human lives in terms of the ability to will the spiritual good cuts across the institutionalizing of inequality in the name of social class and biolgical family. Everyone shall be enabled to become what one has in oneself to become. The options are perpetually open so that at the 'right' time there will be the needed turning around for everyone. This is what is meant by *adhikar*, eligibility.

REFERENCES

1. Robert C. Christopher, *The Japanese Mind: The Goliath Explained* (New York: Linden Press, 1983) pp. 259-64.
2. Edward A. Feigenbaum and Pamela McCorduck, *The Fifth Generation: Artificial Intelligence and Japan's Computer Challenge to the World* (New York: New American Library, 1984) pp. 107-64
3. Toyomasa Fuse ed., *Modernisation and Stress in Japan* (Leiden: E.J. Brill, 1975) p. 39.
4. Jared Taylor, *Shadows of the Rising Sun* (New York: William Morrow, 1983) p. 121.
5. M.J. Wolfe, *The Japanese Conspiracy* (New York: Empire Books, 1983) pp. 167-210.
6. Richard Tanner Pascale and Anthony Pascale. *The Art of Japanese Management* (London: Allen Lane, Penguin Books, 1982) p. 22.
7. Peter F. Drucker, *Management* (London: Heineman, 1974) p. xii.
8. Raimundo Panikkar, *The Vedic Experience* (Delhi: Motilal Banarsidas, 1994) p. 4.
9. Jabala Upanishad, 4.

2

THE VEDIC SYSTEM

Most scholars on Vedic literature know the difference between Vedas and Veda—Vedas refer to the original four Vedas; the Vedas Rig, Vedas Yajur, Vedas Sama and Vedas Atharva—Vedas; Veda, refers to not only the four Vedas, but also to the Upanishads, Vedanta-*Sutras*, Brahmanas and Aranyakas; all the texts are considered to be *Shruti* (that which has to be heard). Shruti is considered to be the original revealed knowledge. The remaining part of the Vedic literature consists of the *Bhagavad Gita* and the *(Dharmashastras*, like the Laws of Manu, Kautilya's *Arthashastra* or the *Smriti* (that which has to be remembered); the *Mahabharata*, the *Ramayana* and Puranas, or the Itihasas or histories and supplemental portions of the Vedic literature (that which represents the historical aspect). Vedic literature refers to both Shruti, Smriti and Itihasas in a general way. In defining the Vedic system the Vedas and to some extent Vedic literature has been referred to illustrate a point.

The Vedas are very ancient and in interpreting them we have to avoid the two extremes of anachronistic and katachronic interpretations. The former means to introduce old and obsolete notions into contemporary situations; the latter means to interpret a thing of the past with the inadequate categories of the present. And yet any reading of the Vedas has to be a reading out of them as much as into them. The connection cannot be a logical one but has to be an existential one.

This existential connection has to be related to modern man: the contemporary human being in his present though transient mood; man as he is just now and for the time being, for soon modern man will be modern no longer. But there is no other key to man other than modern man himself; all other 'men' (whether ancient or in future) are simply abstractions, for they have either already disappeared or have not yet come to be.

Needless to say, not every inhabitant of our planet today is modern man since all cultures are diachronic, and there are many modernities. The modern man in the present context is a secular man, which does not mean that he is not religious or that he has lost the sense of the sacred. The statement means only that his religiousness and even any sense of sacredness he may possess are both tinged with a secular attitude. 'Secular attitude' mean a particular temporal awareness that invests time with a positive and real character. The temporal world is seen as important and the temporal play of man's life and human interaction is taken seriously.

Furthermore, modern man, owing perhaps to the changes that have taken place in human geography and history, can no longer belong to a homogenous or isolated culture. He is bombarded by ideas, images, and sounds from all four corners of the globe. He may have a superficial and even erroneous knowledge of other people, yet cultures mix, ideas intermingle, religions encounter one another, and languages interact and borrow from one another as perhaps never before in human history. The culture of modern man may not be very stable; in fact, he may even be threatened with the loss of all culture, but he is undoubtedly transculturally influenced.

It is important to note, however, that in one respect, that to time, the concept will be 'non-modern'. For the Vedic concept of time is cyclical as opposed to the linear concept held by modern man. The latter provides a linear configuration in terms of a beginning, middle and end in the passage of time. In Vedic thought, however, in the cyclical concept there is no beginning or end, for time is an endless flow moving in ceaseless circles. What appears to be the beginning at one position of the circle is but the end of the previous position. What appears as the end is seen as a new beginning. Time, thus, neither begins nor ends but moves continuously in cycles. This gives to activity an endless and, what may be called in today's world of virtual reality, a seamless flow.

In contrast, the Vedic concept of humanity, is more in line with the views of modern man. For in the Vedas there is, as we shall soon see, stress on the centrality of man, the relativity of all things, on multi-disciplinarity and a multi-cultural world view. This the Vedas do through their methodology of conceiving gods or *devas* as representing various aspects of the one God, both as disciplines and as forces of nature.

The Vedic Methodology

The Vedas have for long been the authority on which all later Hindu systems—economic, political, social—are based. The Vedas being fundamentally a record of experiences of intuition and revelation, the observation of the seers tend to be varied and belong to various stages of human and individual development and exploration. The Vedas record not only the experiences of the poets who have composed the hymns of the Vedas, but also the experiences of the ancestors (*pitarah, poorvajanah*). Vedas thus, describe the knowledge contained in the pre-Vedic tradition as also the Vedic tradition proper.

The Vedas probably took their present shape in the second millennium before Christ, but their roots go back to far more ancient times. Perhaps nowhere else can one observe the whole process of human evolution from its primordial utterance to the most elaborate poetic speech and the most profound philosophy. The Vedas, as we have noted are known as *shruti*, that which has been 'heard': they are not merely the product of human ingenuity but of revelation, that is an 'unveiling' of the truth. They are also called *nitya*, that is 'eternal', signifying that they do not derive from the world of time and change, but are reflections of the eternal. Finally, they are said to be *apaurusheya*, 'without human authorship', they are expressions of the eternal word, the *vak*, and the human authors are *seers* those who have 'seen' the truth, and 'poets' (*kavi*), those whose utterance is inspired.

Here it may be useful to note what the notion of the Vedas having no author, either human or divine, means for us. The theory of there being no author of the Vedas has often been ridiculed as a contradiction of common sense and a denial of causal thinking. The idea of having no author, in my thinkng, seems to imply that at the core of this conception there is a desire to purify man's relationship with the Vedic text. Any one of us is the author of the Vedas when we read, meditate and understand them. Nobody is the author of living words, like those of Vedas, except the one who utters them. The absence of an author means that there is no one who has laid down a relationship between words and their meaning. It is the reader who establishes this relationship thereby making of the Vedas a real or saving knowledge.

This conception, paradoxically enough, rescues the Vedas from the grip not only of a certain God functioning as a primal scribe, but also of the Hindu tradition, which cannot be said to be the author of the Vedas. The Vedas without an author also cease to be "authoritative" books which need to be dogmatically followed. Only when you become their "author", when through assimilation you are able to "hear" them, when you yourself are their proper origin, the author of the text, do the Vedas disclose their authentic "authority".

The fact that the Vedas have no author and thus no anterior authority, the fact that they possess only the value contained in the actual existential act of really "hearing" them, imparts to them a universiality that makes them peculiarly relevant today. They dispose us to listen and then we hear what we hear, trusting that it is also what was to be heard.

This has meant that scholars have extracted from the Vedas perspectives relating, among other things, to Mathematics[1], Ecology[2], the Yogic Origin of Civilization[3],

Mysticism[4], and so on. In line with what other scholars have done, an attempt has been made here to extricate meaning from the Vedic *mantras* or hymns by studying them from a management persepctive.

The Vedas do not propound any single, well defined creed and have given rise to a large number of interpretations and philosophies. But there are some themes in the Vedic teaching which would be relevant to a study of management: The interplay between the 'One' and the 'Many', the unity and the multiplicity and the process by which the many are integrated; the concept of equality; sacrifice as the integrating dynamic of the universe; unification as the journey from the 'Many' to the 'One' through consciouness-raising (also called yoga); and peace as the end to be attained both in the individual and the society.

One and the Many

Since the beginning, a basic question has persisted. "Is the universe monistic or pluralistic?" Whether man is primitive or civilized, illiterate or highly educated, he perceives a pluralistic world, and thus gets *prima facie* evidence of the existence of multiplicity in the world through his five sense-organs[5].

Man saw the vast earth and the infinite sky. He could not estimate the dimensions of the sky, or conceive of the boundaries of space. He could not make out the millions of glaxies. Even our own galaxy (the milky way) was unknown to him. But he could discern the sun, the moon, some planets of our solar system and the innumerable stars in the night sky. He observed diversity on the earth: numerous and scattered mountains, rivers, seas and oceans, hills and valleys. He also noticed diverse forms of life on earth: varieties of human beings, families, genera and species of plants and animals.

Some of the interrelationship between the diverse elements were understood by Vedic man. What he could not understand he attributed to magic, to gods whom he called the possessors of *maya* or magic. According to the function studied, a god was specified. Vedic man correlated gods also to plans of existence or consciousness. The three worlds or planes referred to in the Vedas, being *bhur, bhuvar, swar* (earth, atmosphere, heaven). The Atharva Veda (10.9.12) goes on to say that some of the groups of gods (11 each) are celestial, some are atmospheric and the rest are terrestrial, thus correlating gods to the heavens, atmosphere and the earth.

The large number of gods mentioned in the Vedas has led to controversy among scholars as to whether this concept of the Vedas represents monotheism, polytheism, pantheism, henotheism or 'kathenotheism'. None of the above categories really applies. In the Vedas the worship of many gods has always occurred along with a teaching of the identity of the many gods with the One. This unity is conceived as not only being in the external world but also in the internal workings in man whereby all organs of perception and action are united in a supra-sensual entity. This concept of an underlying unity in nature as well as the human being has led to the development of meditative and yogic practices. The result has been that India has produced a constant stream of sages who sought knowledge of the deeper workings of the mind in mystical states as a means of integrating themselves into holistic personalities.

The Vedic seers are among the more ancient and renowned of these sages of India. The multiplicity of gods in the Vedas and their link with the One has to their vision always reflected not a crude polytheism, pantheism, henotheism or 'kathenotheism' but an abundance of living approaches to the Divine. In this concept, the gods were only meant to perform certain functiosn on behalf of the One.

The Vedic vision of the seers culminates in the great mystical realization "I am the One, I am the Brahman."[6] The Rig Veda (4.26.1) says,

> All this in the beginning was Brahman. It knew itself as I am Brahman. Seeing this, the Rishi Vamadeva realized "I was the father of the human race and I become the Sun".

This realization is much like what Moses heard at the burning bush in the Old Testament, of God as "I am that I am." In the teaching of the Vedas such knowledge is not, however, considered to be the exclusive property of a rare prophet or messiah but is declared to be the heritage and goal of each soul, its own ultimate destiny. It is this concept which has led to the development of various kinds of yoga—whether based on action, devotion, intellect or concentration—as a means of attaining to the One. This has given to humanity the great concept of equality of every human being in the spiritual sense irrespective of the work that anyone performs or the path that is followed.

But though the Vedic seer recognizes the transcendental Being which is the one only, but, in his invocations, he praises and worships the functional gods and not the transcendental Being. The phenomenal universe functions under the control of the One Lord (*Ishwara*) who is another aspect of the Transcendental One in the world of name and form. But as regards the Transcendental One:

> There sight travels not, nor speech, nor the mind[7] and from which words turn away without attaining and the mind also returneth baffled[8].

Since the speech and mind travels not to the One, praise and worship as described in the Veda can obviously be meant for the functional gods only. The functional gods are also described in language by different names in accordance with their attributes and functions. But the functional goes are only different aspects of the One who is "without hue but has obtained manifold hues by His yogic power."[9] Also the One Lord is infinite and has "innumerable heads, eyes and feet which are everywhere".[10]

The Rig Veda in a hymn, the Purusha *Sukta*, the Primal Man, also describes the pervasive nature of the immanent Purusha as one "who possesses a thousand heads, arms and feet" as well as to how the "sacrifice" led to creation.[11] The immanent One, is however, at the same time transcendent:

> Mightier than His might is Purusha,

One-fourth of whom is all that has come into being,
While three-fourths of him resides in the region of immortality.

With three-fourths hath Purusha risen up,

With one-fourth having become again this,

Thence spreading over what eats and does not eat.[12]

The might of Purusha, the indweller God, is expressed in creation, which by virtue of God's presence abides as a self-renewing and enternal process. But, lest one misunderstand that god thus immanent in the world process is not distinct from it, we are immediately reminded that God, the indwelling Purusha, is greater than His might, in the sense that God essentially transcends the world process. It is in His immanent form that all the gods exist and not in His transcendental one.

Deeper probe into the Vedic texts also reveals that in their conception, the various gods are not different from one another although they carry different names. They are only different forms of the same substance just as water and ice are both H_2O. In spite of their apparent differences in identities, according to the Rig Veda the One is identified with gods such as Mitra, Varuna, Yama and Matarishvan.[13] The Atharva Veda (13.3.13) gives a description of Agni in the following way.

Agni becomes Varuna in the evening and Mitra in the morning; becoming Savita he moves through the air and becoming Indra he glows in the middle of the sky.

This hymn is clear about the identity of the Vedic gods; They are different in name, but one in reality. According to the hymn, Agni becomes Varuna; he becomes Mitra, he also becomes Savita and Indra and all the gods are comprehended in him. He encompasses all the gods as the felly rings the spokes is the simile given in a hymn of the Rig Veda (1.141.9) where Agni is invoked,

Through you, O Agni, Varuna enforces the laws, Mitra dispels darkness and Aryama becomes bounteous. And thus all of them are universally comprehended in you in their functions. You encompass them all who are like spokes in a felly.

The Vedic seers thus, poetically describe the single unitary Being as the substrate of the empirical multiple godly entities who are called by different names according to their different attributes and functions. They also become the All. Prana may be taken as an example. In the Atharva Veda, hymn (10.4) has been dedicated to the deity Prana. According to this hymn, the universe is subject to Prana who is the Lord of all and on whom all is supported. He is the Lord of both the living and the non-living creations. He is Viraj; he is Deshta. He is Sun and Moon. He is Prajapati, Matarishvan, Vayu. The past, the future, everything is supported by Prana.

The Vedic surface thus gives a variegated appearance, a mosaic-like scenario with different forms and colours; but beneath the surface is a homogeneous, undifferentiated, unbroken whole, one, non-dual, without a second.

The Rig Veda declares;

Reality (the divine, well-winged Garutmat) is One only, which is verbally expressed by the seers in diverse ways

ekam sadvipra bahudha vadanti (10.164.66).

Also,

The wise seers verbally protray the well-winged Divine Being that exists as One only in many ways

suparnam viprah kavayo vachovirekam shantam bahudha kalpayanti (10.114.5).

The One is spoken of (*vadanti*) by sages or imagined (*kalpayanti*) by poets and seers in different ways.

Unity and Multiplicity

Two questions arise concerning the One and the Many: How did the One become the Many? If there is equality between the One and the Many, how is man to proceed from the empirical Many to a realization in identity with the One?

The first question relates to the devolution or descent of the One into the world of name and form. The second to the return path, the evolution of man into a spiritual being who gets nearer to the One until he finally realizes his identity with the One.

The first question deals with Vedic cosmogony. In the Veda the universe is compared to an inverted tree, with roots above. Below and above spread its branches, nourished by the *gunas;* sense-objects are its buds.[14] The Kathopanisad (2.3.1) also uses the same simile; it compares the world with an inverted tree. An infinitesimally tiny seed germinates; a sprout appears; it grows and becomes the world-tree.

But though Vedic cosmogony uses the simile of vegetative germination, the act of creation starts with ovogenesis. An egg is said to appear in the beginning which thereafter explodes into parts. An excessive quantity of heat is formed as a result of this explosion. The Universe expands and different forms of matter and energy evolve. The expansion will be followed by a contraction. The evolution will be followed by an involution. The whole Universe will come back to the original state of the primaeval egg that will ultimately disappear.

The Vedas declare the formation of the cosmic embryo.[15] The seer of the Upanishad gives a clear description of the formation of the cosmic egg, its subsequent explosion and splitting into two parts.[16] The Vedic cosmogony also refers to the superheated condition that prevails during the period immediately following the explosion of the cosmic egg.[17] The creation of matter and energy would not have been possible without the generation of an excessive quantity of heat.

According to the Upanishads, the expansion of the Universe is brought about through *tapas* or meditation. Meditation, according to the Upanishads, is also the instrumentality through which one attains bliss and fearlessness. Says the Taittirya Upanishad (2.6,7),

> Desiring that he become many, that he should make of himself forms, Brahman mediated. Meditating, he created all things. Creating all things, he entered into everything. Entering into all things, he become that

> which has shape and that which is shapeless; he became that which can be defined and that which cannot be defined; he become that which has support and that which has not support; he become that which is conscious and that which is subtle. He become all things whatsover; therefore the wise call him the Real.
>
> Before creation came into existence, Brahman existed as the Unmanifest. From the Unmanifest he created the Manifest. From himself he brought forth himself. Hence he is known as Self-Existent. The Self-Existent is the essence of all Beatitude. For who could live, who could breathe, if that blissful Self dwelt not within the lotus of the heart? He it is that gives joy. When a man finds his existence and unity in the Self—who is the basis of life, who is beyond all predicates—then alone does he transcend fear. So long as there is the least idea of separation from him, there is fear. To the man who thinks himself learned, yet knows not himself as Brahman, Brahman, who drives away all fear, appears as fear itself.

But the realization of Brahman, of the unity is not so easy even if we know how the One became many. For this to come about our individualized nature needs to live in the single consciousness of an inner and outer movement dedicated to something that is beyond us and greater than ourselves. In all action there must be a consciousness that we are presenting it to the one divine Being who is also in all beings. This is the way of the absence of hate and grief, or putting it positively, to love and happiness. Says the Isha Upanishad (6, 7).

> He who sees all beings in the One, and the One in all beings, hates none.
>
> To the illumined soul, the One is all. For he who sees everywhere oneness, how can there be delusion or grief.

The Veda has always considered perception of the One as knowledge and perception of the many as ignorance. But the Veda has never considered ignorance or knowledge of the many as irrelevant to life. To turn again to the Isha Upanishad (9, 10, 11),

> To darkness are they doomed who devote themselves only to the ignorance (life in the world), and to a greater darkness they who devote themselves only to the knowledge (meditation on the One).
>
> Life in the world alone leads to one result, meditation alone leads to another. So have we heard from the wise.
>
> They who devote themselves both to life in the world (the Many) and to meditation (the One), by life in the world overcome death and by meditation achieve immortiality.

The Veda does not demand rejection of the world of plurality but the attaining of harmony between the inward poise and the outward action. This is the path to the psycho-social integration of man and the creation, of harmony between his inner self and the outer world: The management of oneself leads to management of the external environment.

Sacrifice in the Veda

In one had to choose a single word to express the quintessence of the Vedic Revelation, the word *yagya*, sacrifice, would perhaps be the most adequate. Sacrifice is, in fact, an ancient, far-reachig and pervasive intuition of the Vedas. The basic characteristic of sacrifice seems to be that of an action that reaches where it intends to reach, that really and truly offers something, that stretches out and extends itself. In other words, sacrifice seems to suggest an action that effectively 'creates', that is, it acts, is efficient and produces what it intends.

The law of life as sacrifice is a very profound idea which was universal in the ancient world. It appears in the Veda and the basis of the whole Vedic system is that everything comes from and must return to, the Creator. Sacrifice being the law of the universe man has to perform this rite of return and the sacrifice is that act by which he restores things to god. In making everything over to the Divine through sacrifice, man is fulfilling the law of the universe and he, correspondingly, is himself fulfilled. By this practice, all his desires are met. So sacrifice is not primarily negative. We tend to think of sacrifice as giving up something, but that is really only a preliminary aspect. The deeper meaning is that we take things out of our own use and make them over to God.

In this sense the law of sacrifice is the common divine action that was thrown out into the word in its beginning as a symbol of the solidarity of the universe. It is by the attraction of this law that a divine saving power descends to limit and correct and gradually to eliminate the errors of an egoistic and self-divided humanity. Also to satisfy all desires including the realization of the One. For with sacrifice as their companion, says the *Bhagavad Gita*, the Lord of Creation created these people so that all their desires could be fulfilled.[18]

The acceptance of the law of sacrifice is a practical recognition by the human ego that it is neither alone in the world nor the centre of the universe. It is an admission by the ego that, even in this much fragmented existence, there is beyond itself and behind that which is not its own egoistic person, something greater and completer, a diviner One which demands from it subordination and service. Indeed sacrifice is imposed and where need be, compelled by the universal World-Force; It takes it even from those who do not consciously recognize the law—inevitably, because this is the intrinsic nature of things. For the truth is, that the ego which thinks itself a separated independent being and claims to live for itself, is not independent and separate but rather linked together with others by a Oneness.

The attainment of the true unity is not only an association and agglomeration for the attainment of common interests; it is not even an emotional understanding, sympathy and solidarity. To be really unified with those separated from us we have to annul the division and become one with what we considered to be not ourselves. As the Isha Upanishad (6,7,8) says:

> He who sees all beings in the Self, and Self in all beings.

> ...to whom the Self is all, who sees everywhere oneness, there is no delusion or grief?
>
> The Self is everywhere...he it is that has established perfect order among objects and beings from beginningless time.

It is in this perception of the Unity that the sacrifice has to be made...of one's ego, desires and objectives.

In the Purusha Sukta hymn of the Rig Veda (referred to earlier) there is the sacrifice and dismemberment of the cosmic Person (the Purusha); and that is what leads to creation. Since He, the Purusha, was the only One, He had to use His own body in a sacrifice to create the universe. The hymn goes on to refer to Purusha, the primeval cosmic being, as the source and origin not only of the physical universe but also of religion and the social order. Quite clearly everything in this world was perceived as being bodily related to the divine source, the body of God.

In later verses of the hymn[19], the Purusha sacrifices himself by dismembering Himself and scattering around the necessary number of portions for the completion of the work of creation. He performs an act of self-immolation so that the universe may come into being. From this sacrifice offered completely, that is, from His limbs, come all things both animate and inanimate: Animals of every type (8, 10); liturgical formulas (9); the four castes of men (12); the cosmic powers (13-14). From His spirit comes the moon, from His eyes the sun, from His mouth Indra and Agni (fire), from His breath the wind, from His navel the air, from His head the sky, from His feet the earth, from the ears the points of the compass—nothing, nobody, is omitted. Verse 15 sums up the idea of the sacrifice and the last stanza repeats the underlying thought of the whole hymn, that the cosmic Man is the total sacrifice.

The sacrifice of the cosmic Man signifies divine transcendence investing humanity. This universal sacrifice possesses a twofold dynamism, for it includes a sacramental downward movement of the All toward the earth and a sacrificial upward movement of the world toward the All; these two aspects are inseparable from each other precisely because of the unity of the integral sacrifice.

In the above myth of the Purusha we have the Vedic principle that creation and creativity, requires a sacrifice: Of the body, the egoistic impulses, of looking at oneself as the centre of the universe. It is the 'sacrifice' of oneself that leads to creativity not the closing in of everything on one's ego: A principle that in management terms leads to laying stress on teamwork and trust in others rather than on ego-centred and centralized, control and direction.

The Vedic sacrifice is undergirded by an important symbol. This symbol is *rita*. As its etymology suggests *rita* stands for the principle of order and of the activity.[20] *Rita* is the very energy of the sacrifice; it is what tiggers the sacrifice. Austerity, truth, and *rita* share an intimate relationship.[21] Truth without *rita* would not be true. The powers of austerity, concentration, energy and the like are connected with *rita*. Indeed, the whole order of the universe is said to come from and be maintained by the dynamism of *rita*.

Rita is generally translated as 'cosmic order', which is a valid translation provided one bears in mind that cosmic order is not a fixed physical or mathematical law, but a 'sacrificial' order. In the words of the Rig Veda itself: Cosmic order is maintained by sacrificial order; that is, *rita* is upheld by *rita*.[22] *Rita* is the ultimate foundtion of everything; it is 'the supreme', although this is not to be understood in a static sense. *Rita* it is that creates order out of chaos.

The Rig Veda has this to say of *rita*:

> Firm-seated are the foundations of *rita*, in its lovely form are many splendid beauties.
>
> By *rita* they give us long-lasting nurture; by *rita* have the worlds entered the universal order.[23]

We see in the above verse the interlinking of beauty and order. In the Vedic view, the attempt to reduce chaos through *rita* itself produces beauty which is an inextricable part of world order. The idea is that only from the godhead, who is conceived as the fountain of truth, goodness and beauty, can good come, evil be dispersed and order created out of chaos. *Rita* has, in the Vedic concept, also connotations of a moral code, of aesthetic beauty and of social order. In its moral aspects, *rita* comes very close to being synonymous with the later concept of *dharma*.

The earth, according to the Atharva Veda, is upheld by *dharman* (referred to as *dharma* in later ages)[24] and in another verse the same Veda (12.11) refers to the earth being upheld by truth, order, consecration, austerity, prayer and sacrifice.

> Truth, order that is stern, consecration, austerity, prayer and sacrifice—these uphold the earth.
>
> May that earth, the mistress of our past and future, make a wide world for us.

It needs to be noted that none of the gods or God, are mentioned in the above verse as the upholder of earth, that function being left to eternal law and other qualities of an ethical nature.

The transition from the One to the Many is, as we have seen, through sacrifice, sacrifice which is dynamised by *rita* or order. The reverse movement, from the Many to the One, requires the awakening of human consciousness, like the awakening into life, as a process of sifting and discrimination. Growth implies and requires differentiation, separations, a self-affirmation by a negation of the other, a looking into oneself, and a concern with what is happening within one's self, all concentrated in the internal process of finding the self that exists precisely because it has been set apart from other selves and thus from the totality.

This is the horizontal vision whereby man discovers himself and his own projection into the outer world. For though the individual is biologically a single specimen of the human species, he is a part of the whole and even when he acquires conciouness of the surrounding world and a certain awareness of himself as a different and peculiar element in the whole, he is not yet a person. He can function as a human being only if society takes care of him and he conforms to the given pattern. In other words, the individual can act and behave as a human being if there is a colllectivity, a higher 'person', of which he is a part and on behalf of which he performs the acts he is required to do. This superior person can be the family, the tribe, the sect, the religious community, the region, the nation, or any other group that encompasses the whole of human existence.

The individual thus becomes a person when he discovers that he is an unrepeatable complex of relations, a unique knot in a net of relationships; he becomes a person when his individual consciousness becomes aware of being neither a subject looking out upon an objective world nor an object being looked upon and also looked after, by a superior authority, but when he discovers that he himself is subject and object at the same time, that he himself is the whole insofar as the whole is mirrored in him and passes through him.

In making the transition from an undeveloped human life to full personhood, the first sign of coming of age is not a biological change but a psychological realization: The discovery of the other as a mysterious part of oneself; the realization that he or she is neither onself nor an 'other' and much less another self. This is the first and personal discovery; the discovery that makes a human being a person. It is the discovery of the relationship of love, in which the other is not an instrument (to be manipulated according to one's own wishes) or a 'thing', on obstacle or an enemy, but the beloved, the thou, and—ultimately—the I. This link with something 'superior' to oneself through love, or yoga, is what makes an individual a 'whole' person. It is in this context that the Vedic sages conceived of society as a unifying force.

The Vedic Society

While unifying the various deities in their own subtle and unique way, the Vedic seers could not ignore the need for unifying and stablizing society. A potent force sundering Vedic society was the ongoing conflict between the Aryan and non-Aryan peoples. In the Rig Veda we find many references to the antipathy between the Aryan and the Dasyu (the non-Aryan people) becoming muted and transformed with the passage of time. The early references in the Vedic verses make contemptuous references to the dark skinned and unlawful Dasas (another name for the Dasyus) who are 'followers of evil laws, inhuman, riteless, godless'[25]. Later on the difference between the Arya and the Dasyu is not seen as one between peoples and tribes but as between enlightment and ignorance, between goodness and wickedness, between the lawful and the unlawful. The goal becomes one of eliminating the evil-doer even if he is 'one of us' and not of a tribe or people. The two verses from the Rig Veda reproduced below reflect this change.

He (Indra) is the holder of the thunderbolt,

destroyer of the Dasyu, fearful and mighty. (1.100.12)

Whatever evil-doer wants to kill us,

Whether he is a stranger or one of us,

May all gods discomfit him,

My prayer is a coat of mail within me (6.75.1).

In Vedic thought, the agent of evil, the evil-doer has to be destroyed even if he is a kinsman,—'one of us.' It was for this reason that in the *Bhagavad Gita* Sri Krishna told Arjuna at Kurukshetra to kill his wicked kinsmen, for not to do so, would be un-Aryan.[26] The Atharva Veda carries this thought further and suggests leaving the evil-doers and crossing over to those who are good.

The stream, filled with stones, flows on,

move together,

And quit you like heroes and cross over, my friends

Leave here those who are evil-minded,

Let us cross over to powers that are beneficient.[27]

The whole perception, therefore, shifts from 'us' and

'they', 'Arya' and 'Dasyu', to good and evil, the righteous and the unrighteous. From this it is but a small step for the Rig Veda to assert that 'the Lord God of glory is He to whom both the Arya and the Dasa belong'[28] and to ask for forgiveness from Varuna for sins committed against neighbours and foreigners.

> If, Varuna, we have sinned against the man who loves us or against a friend,
>
> Or a comrade for ever, or a brother,
>
> Or against a neighbour who is always with us
>
> or against a foreigner,
>
> From that sin may Thou release us.[29]

The differences between the Arya and the Dasyu were not only removed on the conceptual and thinking planes but social grouping was also done on the basis of a unifying principle. Society was divided into four types of persons, or orders, on the basis of functions and attributes; brahmin, the man of knowledge and religion; kshatriya, the man of politics and warfare; vaishya, the man of industry and trade; and shudra, the working man. All could be members of these orders or classes irrespective of the tribe or race to which they belonged. To unify the four orders, it was stated that they had all originated from the Purusha.

> The man of knowledge (brahmin) was His mouth, His arms were made the man who manage (kshatriya);
>
> His thigs were that which is the man of trade (vaishya), out of His feet was born the working man (shudra).[30]

Later distortions of the four orders which degenerated into the caste system, including its rigid stratification, colour much of the modern view of it. There is no doubt, however, that in the circumstances of the times, the concept of four orders prevented a great deal of bloodshed and civil strife, if not genocide, unified society by making every order spiritually have the same source, making righteousness the path for all to follow and led to the orderly development of Indian civilization and culture.

The heroes of the Aryans, a militant tribe, were the

indomitable warriors, the kshatriyas, whose field of activity in the system was the conduct of war and the extension of the territories of the State. The brahmins, on the other hand, were the contemplative minds intent on harmonizing all conflicts and disharmonies. The way of the brahmins was the way of the mystics and the philosophers, and their search was for the unifying principle underlying all phenomena (much like the manner in which Einstein spent the last years of his life researching in the sphere of the unified field). Whereas to the kshatriyas, foreigners and other races and tribes were meant to be conquered; to the Vedic sages God was as much for foreigners as for their own people.

> God (Varuna) is That in which things converge.
>
> He is That from which things diverge,
>
> He is of our own land, He is of foreign land,
>
> He is divine, He is human.[31]

In other ways also there were disharmonies between the two views, of those of the men of action and those of the men of contemplation. The Puranas relate how Parashuram, the warrior brahmin, shattered the power of kshatriyas several times to bring them back to the path of the rightful law. In the end, however, the two kinds of men and the two faculties of the mind, those of contemplation and of action, had to be synthesizd and harmonized. Coexistence of the two kinds of power, whether externally in society or internally within man, was declared the norm rather than an ongoing conflict. The Yajur Veda prays for the strengthening of knowledge and the strengthening of valour[32] and would like the world to be such that spiritual power and ruling power can move together in harmony.[33] The Veda also calls for lustre to be given to both *brahmins* and *kshatriyas*.

> Give lustre to our men of holy lore, give lustre to our kingly men.[34]

The Way of Dharma

The concept of the four orders had to be harmonized in a spiritual manner. This the Vedic sages did through the concept of *rita* and *dharma*. One of the dominant ideas flowing from the Vedic revelation has been that of *dharma* or righteousness. According to the Vedic sages, *dharma* had to be discovered by each individual and could not be formulated in the form of rigid law. Flowing as *dharma* or *rita* did from the concept of sacrifice, certain universal harmonies could be discovered through sacrifice of one's ego to become guidelines of action. Many of these guidelines are to be found in the Veda itself, and they are expressed, tacitly or explicitly, as revelations and given to people in their varying capacities of receptivity as direct lines of approach to the truth either through a discipline or spiritual practice or through symbolism or through the concept of sacrifice. The end aimed at is to know the Veda, to speak the truth.

> May you, speech and mind, bring to me the wisdom of the Veda. May I speak the truth of Brahman. May I speak the truth.[35]

It is from this formulation that the later idea of *dharma* grew and developed. As the original idea of *rita* could never be rigidly fixed, even so, there could not be any one fixed formulation of *dharma*. In a certain sense, *dharma* has always remained some indefinable thing. Thus, although *dharma* has been upheld as the highest non-legislative law which even the highest political authorities had to obey, one fixed and uniform formulation of *dharma* is nowhere to be found.

Indeed, there have been several formulations and in many respects these formulations have been in conflict with each other, and attempts have been made throughout history to reconcile this conflict in some flexible and synthetic formulation of law. The great Smritis[36] of Yajnavalkaya and Manu are attempts to codify this *dharma*, and although these two are themselves in conflict with each other in many respects, they have provided a general background of a common formulation of the basic idea of *dharma*. But this codification itself was never regarded as absolute, and although in later times they came to be applied rigidly, there were always supervening claims of the unformulated *dharma*. In fact, we find in most catholic teachings such as those of the *Bhagavad Gita* an injunction to transcend all *dharmas* and to surrender to the highest Truth and to the Supreme One. Sri Krishna says to Arjuna:

> Abandon all *dharmas*, come to Me alone for shelter. Be not grieved, for I shall release thee from all ills.[37]

Dharma is more a guideline than law or dogma. The idea is to prevent human beings from giving in to unrestrained demands of impulses, desires, ambitions and egoisms. That is why, Vedic culture enjoined upon individuals to restrain the desire for enjoyment and personal profit by following *dharma*. Thus, we find the prevalent idea that *kama* and *artha*, enjoyment and personal gain, the primary motives for the ordinary man, are not ends in themselves. *Kama* and *artha* are to be superseded and controlled by *dharma*. The individual has to grow out of passions, impulses, and selfish and egoistic interests if he is to reach the ideal law of *dharma*.

It is this idea of *dharma* that lies behind the governing ideas that determined the organization of the varied aspects of Vedic life. Fundamentally, it gave rise to the predominant tendency to place the law of the truth as the sole law to which the individual and society are called upon to give their ultimate allegiance. Thus, there came about in Vedic society an organization of human life in which each individual and collectivity was given the freedom to develop in accordance with the law of the truth; the state could legislate, but the legislation had to be in accordance with and subservient to, the law of the truth. This is what is meant by the law of *dharma* and this is the significance of the superiority that was ascribed to *dharma* in determining the individual and collective life. Says the Taittiriya Upanishad (1.11),

> Speak the truth, follow the *dharma*.

But *dharma* is not, according to Vedic thought, the highest stage or motive of human life. For one thing *dharma* is not something fixed or rigid. And even if in the initial stages the pursuit of *dharma* is guided by some fixed and acceptable code of conduct, the individual has to discover *swadharma*[38], one's own specific law of self-development based on one's unique psycho-social personality. For Vedic culture recognizes that every individual has his own specific *dharma*, the peculiar law of growth appropriate to his functions and flowing out of his qualities and capacities. Thus, the search for *dharma* has to be a life of inner search, a life of self-knowledge, and its harmonization with the outer actions and activities.

The individual is asked and allowed to follow his *swadharma* to its own extreme limit. It is when the end is reached that the individual discovers that real truth and spiritual stuff of himself and also the spiritual way of action. This is the inner meaning of spiritual liberation, or *moksha*, which is placed before the individual as the supreme aim of life.

But though *moksha* is considered the ultimate goal, Vedic thought also recognizes the need for following the path of prosperity. On the face of it the two paths—the material and the spiritual—seem to go in opposite directions: One is marked by selfishness, the other by selflessness; one seeks to possess and the other to renounce. But the two have been conceived by the Veda as being complementary and not competitive. As the Isha Upanishad (1, 2) says,

> In the heart of all things, of whatever there is in the universe, dwells the Lord. By renouncing desire thou shouldest enjoy; lust not after any man's possession.
>
> Doing verily works in this world one should wish to live a hundred years. Thus it is, and not otherwise, that action cleaves not to a man.

It is thus inner renunciation (*tyaga*) that is called for and not abstention from the path of prosperity and pleasure. Sri Krishna in the *Bhagavad Gita* (2.47) carries the matter further when he says,

> To action alone thou hast the right and never at all to its fruits; let not the fruits of action by thy motive; neither let there be in thee any attachment to inaction.

Desireless action (*nishkama karma*) is the way to liberation not the giving up of action. Sri Krishna later on in the *Bhagavad Gita* (18.2) again clarifies that "understand by 'renunciation' the giving up of works prompted by desire".

Fully conscious of the mighty hold that the material attractions of the world have on human minds, the Vedic seers formulated a social scheme that had a place both for seekers of temporal well-being as well as for the seekers of spiritual values. So the Vedic system has two distinct courses: (i) The way of activity (*pravritti-marga*), and (ii) the way of renunciation (*nivritti-marga*), characterized respectively by desire and desirelessness. The former is intended to lead to plenty and pleasure here and hereafter, whereas the latter is intended to lead to the Supreme. Manu, a well-known codifier of the Vedic rules of life, remarks:

> Activity (*pravritti*) and renunciation (*nivritti*) are the two forms of the Vedic discipline for the attainment of prosperity and happiness and for the attainment of supreme bliss.[39]

The guiding principle of the way of activity is the practice of *dharma*. In the search for wealth, or in the search for pleasure, the seeker should by no means deviate from the moral course. Renunciation, as already pointed out, does not necessarily mean giving up all activities and possessions. Primarily, it is a dispassionate attitude to the temporal consequent on spiritual awakening, that is to say, the turning of the mind to the eternal. The main condition for the way of renunciation is freedom from desires for all that is transitory and a longing for the Eternal. One can have both internal and external renunciation, or only internal. External renunciation without the internal has no value. A person may have the spirit of renunciation even though living in the family. He can be in the world without being worldly-minded.

Through the discipline of the way of outer activity (*pravritti-marga*) a man can gain affluence and happiness not only in this world but also in the worlds beyond. He can strive for merit adequate to reach the very climax of temporal glory and enjoyment after death. This means an immeasurably long term of life in the highest realm of sense-fulfillment, such as a celestial paradise. But he cannot reside there forever. Having experienced the joys and splendours of the heaven-world (*svargoloka*) for a long, long period, until the merit that leads him there is exhausted, he comes back to this earth. Or, he may go farther down to a lower region in consequence of the severe demerit fructifying at the time.

The Mundaka Upanishad (1.2.10) says:

> Deluded persons regarding sacrificial rites and humanitarian deeds to be the highest do not know any higher good (the means of liberation). Having enjoyed (the fruits of their good deeds) on the heights of heaven attainable by meritorious work, they enter again this world or go to an inferior one.

Pravritti and *nivritti* are very significant terms. They are also interpreted as 'turning on the ego' and 'turning away from the ego.' *Parvritti*, then, implies ego-centredness and *nivritti* surrendering the ego, that is, God-centredness.

For world order and security both the ways are essential. Both of them are as old as mankind. They exist side by side. Without the way of activity the way of renunciation cannot function. And the former, unless directed to the latter, cannot hold its own. It goes out of bounds and disrupts life, individual and social. It is a truism that man's sense-appetites are insatiable. They grow and multiply indefinitely, unless well regulated. The two ways of Vedic *dharma* are, as it were, the centrifugal and the centripetal forces that make the human world rightly run its course.

Peace and Fearlessness

The Vedic sages are thus positive in their acceptance of *dharma* and *rita*, the eternal law, of life and death and of life's struggles and imperfections. Being intensely religious, their wishes for the good things of life took the form of ardent prayers for strength, valour, manliness, fearlessness, vigour, intellectual power, wisdom and spiritual vigour.

> O Varuna! sharpen the intelligence, wisdom and insight of him who is striving for enlightenment.[40]
>
> O Hero! give manly vigour to our men.[41]

One thing that the Vedas stress more than anything else is peace. Man may possess everything: health, wealth, wife and children, knowledge and skill, power and glory; but still he can be the most miserable creature if he is lacking that gift of the Gods which does not depend on any other gift and on which all other gifts depend if they are to be real blessings for man—peace. Human fullness is incomplete without peace, whereas even the one who lacks everything else can still have peace within himself and peace with all beings, which in fact constitutes happiness. The Vedas were deeply aware of this and thus of the constant necessity to invoke peace with all the power of the hymns.

The *shanti* hymns or invocation of peace is an essential utterance at any beginning and especially at the end of a sacred action or of the recitation of a sacred text. How can a holy word be uttered or heard unless there is peace in heaven, on earth and in the human heart? The discord and dissonances in the universe and among men have first to be pacified before any real, that is, sacred, act can take place. Here is what the Atharva Veda (19.9.1,2) says,

> Peaceful be heaven, peaceful the earth,
> Peaceful the broad space between.
> Peaceful for us be the running waters,
> Peaceful the plants and herbs!
> Peaceful to us be the signs of fortune,
> Peaceful what is done and undone.
> Peaceful to us be what is and what will be.
> May all to us be gracious!

The Vedas conceive of peace as an undivided whole which has to pervade the whole of nature before it impacts the mind of man. The Katha Upanishad (3.13) carries the matter further by calling "the Self of man as that which is always still and at peace".

In Vedic thought the way to attaining peace is though fearlessness, through the joy that comes from fearlessness. Fear is neverthless one of the congenital diseases of mankind. When the crude and primitive dread of nature is overcome, other forms of fear creep into the human mind and heart and in spite of theological distinctions, the fear of God is still fear. Modern man may no longer fear nature or God, but he is not easily rid of the fear of his fellows nor of that most insidious of all fears, the fear that is a mixture of fear of oneself and fear of nothingness.

> Lead us to a wide world, O wise one, to heavenly light, fearlessness, and blessing.
> Strong are your arms, O powerful Lord.
> We resort to your infinite refuge.
> May the atmosphere we breathe breathe fearlessness into us: fearlessness on earth and fearlessness in heaven!
> May fearlessness guard us behind and before!
> May fearlessness surround us above and below!
> May we be without fear of friend and foe!
> May we be without fear of the known and the unknown!
> May we be without fear by night and by day!
> Let all the world be my friend![42]

The structural similarity of the prayer for fearlessness to the one for peace quoted earlier is striking. This stress upon fearlessness as a human value of capital importance and a sign of personal self-realization is maintained not only in the field of martial courage but also and mainly, in the realm of human perfection. We read, for instance in one Upanishad:

> "Certainly, Janaka, you have achieved fearlessness"
>
> —said Yajnavalkya.
>
> "May fearlessness by with you, Sir!"
>
> —replied Janaka of Videha,[43]

While in another Upanishad we find the vivid metaphor: "the further shore of fearlessness."[44] That shore is the heaven of perfection which we only attain when we practise and are surrounded by universal friendship for that is what drives away fear. Says the Upanishad: "In the heavenly world there is no fear."[45]

The Vedic Approach

The approach of the Vedas to all questions is one of synthesizing opposites, even those that appear at first sight to be irreconcilable. In addition to their positive view of life, the Vedic sages believed passionately in harmonizing the different facets of life, whether external or internal to man and whether of concepts, principles or religions. They accepted as axiomatic the existence of what in modern jargon would be called the antiforces. But they considered these oppsites, whether of lawlessness to law, *adharma* to *dharma*, or of truth to untruth, as the reverse and obverse of a coin rather than as two independent and mutually antagonistic forces. Since they looked at life in all its fullness, the attempt of the Vedic sages was to prevent the loss of balance between the primary biological instincts (struggle for existence, search for food, sex) and the mental and spiritual urges of man; to harmonize the active and contemplative faculties of the mind; and to harmonise the external with the internal, the world of matter with the world of the spirit. The result is that nowhere in Vedic thought we find any evidence of the tragedy of the divided soul, of the dichotomy between different levels of consciousness, or any suggestion that could lead to repression of the primary human instincts. The negative, almost nihilistic, tendencies that in later ages made their appearance in Indian thought and society are conspicuous by there absence in the Vedic scheme of things. Nor do we find the anomie or weariness that usually accompanies world-weary or materially satiated cultures and societies. There is on the other hand, a certain bubbling freshness and an effervescent *joie de vivre* in everything that the Vedic system professes.

The Vedic system is not only positive in its acceptance

of life, with all its limitations and imperfections, but also in its comprehension of the ultimate values of truth, goodness and beauty, of eternal law, and of the one Existence that sages call by many names. The system encourages the development of an intensely religious attitude whereby one can feel the living presence of the Divine in the beauty, vastness and glory of the universe and take joy in the things on earth as well as in the heavens, in the bubbling streams, the lofty mountains, the stars, the sunrises and the sunsets. Strong urges of divine love and reverence and giving vent to feelings in song and poetry, are encouraged and the system exalts the role of the poet over that of the thinker.

Since the system encourages expression through the emotions rather than the mind, Vedic poetry is of a radiant and ecstatic kind 'like joyous streams bursting from the mountain'[46]. It overflows with love of life and is virbant with energy waiting to be harnessed for action. Serenely, and with faith, the Vedic sages looked to the Divine for inspiration and willingly placed themselves under the rule of *tapas, rita, dharma* and truth so that with purified minds and understanding they could delve into the ultimate principles of the universe.

The approach of the Vedic system of thought is a synthetic one. It seeks to harmonize the world of spirit with that of matter. In the social sphere, it lays down the basis of an equitable order in which attainments and function, rather than birth or race, determine the social status of an individual. The system did away with the antipathy between the Arya and the Dasyu, the Aryan and the non-Aryan, while simultaneously harmonizing the Aryan and non-Aryan deities and bringing them under the sway of the eternal verities of truth, goodness and beauty. The Vedic ritual, being the same for all deities was, in addition to the concept of the One called by many names, a unifying factor between the different gods and goddesses. The system also stood for harmony between the economic, political and spiritual forces and the Vedic sages made this the ideal to be aimed at, whether by the individual or by society.

The methodology by which the system attained the various harmonies was by the subtle and non-violent method of retaining names and forms while simultaneously changing the spirit and inner content, whether of deities or of principles. This synthesizing methodology of the Vedic system has been the distinguishing characteristic of Indian culture and civilization and has given to it a dynamism which through the ages has enabled it to absorb new ideas and impulses in a creative and evolutionary manner. This has been the strength of Indian civilization enabling it to withstand various shocks during the last few millennia and to emerge with renewed energy and strength after every such synthesis.

Vedic Thought and Management

Management, be it of a kingdom, a war or a business enterprise has to be based on a value system which gives it a strong foundation. It forms a core, a central focal credo around which people can rally and feel motivated. That management is successful where the value system is so strong and rich that people love to identify themselves with it and give its objectives their wholehearted cooperation. A management to which people rally for personal gains or out of a mere sense of loyalty is like a house of cards, apparently magnificent and succesful, but capable of being scattered in an adverse wind.

Management based on Vedic thought has of necessity to be based on the values inherent in the Vedic system: the dynamism inherent in the sacrifice leading to the concept of selfless behaviour; the importance of *rita* and *dharma*, of a law which creates order out of chaos and syntheizes the Many into the One; of the need for the harmonizing with others even when they are enemies (or competitors in the business sense) if they are ethically akin to us; of working in joy and fearlessness as a way to peace and co-operative behaviour.

Management based on Vedic thought, thus, values cooperation over competition and tries to harmonize its multiple objectives (profit, welfare of society, conservation of the environment, synergy with everyone whether customers, suppliers or competitors) through *rita* and *dharma*.

This is very well illustrated by the Vedic myths concerning the gods or *devas*. As we know, a myth is a symbolic utterance which arises from the depths of the unconscious, or rather from the deep levels of consciousness. The rational mind, with its abstract concepts and logical constructions, is like the tip of an iceberg, while below it are vast levels of consciousness which link our human nature with the universe around us and with the archetypes or transcendent principles which govern the Universe. The myth is the reflection in the human imagination of these archetypal ideas, those cosmic principles and powers, which were known in the ancient world as the gods, angels or *devas*.

Many hypotheses about the gods have been put forward: The idea of the Vedic gods as cosmic powers; of the Vedic gods being mere expressions of the human psyche; of there being one God with sundry little gods acting as his serving spirit; and so on. From a management point of view, the view is best expressed in the Rig Veda (1.164.39):

He who knows not the eternal
syllable of the Veda,
the highest point upon which
all the Gods repose,
what business has he with the Veda?
Only its knowers
sit here in peace and concord.

Knowledge of the gods whether as adjuncts of the One or as powers of Nature or whatever becomes necessary to have "peace and concord", leads to a unified management perspective which is in harmony with the individual, nature and society.

Creation

The Myth of Creation is another one of the great myths of the Vedas. Says the Rig Veda (10.129.1-4):

There was neither Non-existence nor Existence,
Nor was there the Earth or Sky beyond,
What was the covering, whence, and at whose shelter,
Was there the primeval water with depth unfathomed?
Death was not then, nor was there Immortality,
There was no sign of day and night,
That One in the breathless space breathed on its own,
Apart from that there was nothing whatever.
Darkness at the beginning was covered with darkness,
and this All was indiscriminated chaos;
All was then in the Void contained, only the One
hath emerged with its mighty radiance.
Thence arose primal desire in the beginning,
the first seed of the Mind;
Wise sages searched into the heart of mystery,
and found Existence's kinship in Non-existence.[47]

The subject of the above hymn is creation: What existed before creation started and how creation took place. The underlying sense seems to be that absolute transcendence must transform itself into a pure immanence so that creation may emerge out of it, a point more directly expressed in a number of other hymns where the diversity of the universe is related to the One.[48] The creation hymn states that the One, the transcendent, is not directly involved in the creative process. In fact, while the One is—that is, simply abides as one—no creation can take place, and as a result, there are none of the oppositions that arise within creation, such as existence and non-existence, death and immortality, earth and sky, day and night Creation is the process of the One's expansion into the 'all', which at this stage is contained in the void, of the primeval procreative waters, 'the darkness covered with darkness' of the undifferentiated chaos. The One's mighty radiance, "the fulfilling energy up yonder," gives rise to the first form, which is desire arising from within the void of the waters.

As we reflect on this hymn, there emerges something that is of significance for management: that the One becomes Many through the arising of desire. As we shall see later, the reverse process, or the giving up of desire, is the way to integrate the Many into the One, making desirelessness one of the instruments of self-realization and integration of the various aspects of man into a holistic being. This is also the way in which the multidimensional objective function of management can be harmonized into a integrated unity. This is the yogic way very much elaborated in the Upanishads and the *Bhagavad Gita*.

Love

Another value very much stressed by the Vedas is love. *Kama*, or love, as we have already seen is considered to be the first principle of activity, the creative and procreative forces leading the supreme Being out of the closed circle of its own existence. It is a cosmic force, but not to be understood as a kind of blind energy or impersonal urge. On the contrary, the personal is so much included in the transpersonal element that *kama* is said to be the first seed of mind, the firstborn of the Absolute and thereafter the loftiest of human beings. *Kama* is the driving force in any enterprise, the highest of all human qualities. There is one and the same urge stimulating the entire range of reality, one and the same energy pushing the universe to expand—and it is *kama*. Without it there would be only death; time would shrink and reality would collapse. *Kama* is not a hankering after what is lacking in the individual; it is not an imperfection and thus a cause of suffering. *Kama* is not the proof that we have not yet arrived, that we are imperfect and enmeshed in unfulfilled longings and unsatisfied urges. *Kama* is, on the contrary, the perfection of expansion, the quality of creativity, the positive dynamism to be more, to reach higher, to overcome what still stands in front of us, because the adventure of existence is not yet finished, although this unfinished character is just the opposite of the imperfect. A 'finished' universe would be in fact finished, limited, finite, deadly, and not divine. *Kama* proves not that we are poor pilgrims, still on the way, displaced persons in search of a paradise lost, but that we are divine sparks full of creative energy with our own part to play in the structuring of the world.

This is what the Atharva Veda (10.2.19, 25) has to say:

Love is the firstborn, loftier than the Gods,
the Fathers and men.
You, O *Kama*, are the eldest of all,
To you we pay homage!
In many of form of goodness, O *Kama*,
you show your force.
Grant that those forms may penetrate
within our hearts
Send elsewhere all malice!

The absence of malice, of love for all, is the preferred way of advance and the way in which management leads to self-fulfilment of both itself and the individuals comprising it.

The myth of the Purusha has already been dealt with. In this myth, consciousness is not considered as different from Nature or matter. Science is also now slowly recovering the knowledge, which was universal in the ancient world, that there is no such thing as matter apart from mind or consciousness. Consciousness is latent in every particle of matter and the mathematical order which science discovers in the universe is due to the working of this universal consciousness in it.[49] In human nature this latent consciousness begins to come into actual consciousness, and as human consciousness develops it grows more and more grounded. The link between humanity and Nature, is thus, through the universal consciousness which manifests itself when the embodied being is sacrificed. Out of this myth has grown the concept of 'giving up of wants' as a sacrifice and so a way of realizing the original state of consciousness or unity.

Vedic management, thus, is deeply embedded in a value system which tries to integrate the worlds of matter and of spirit; which regards selflessness and cooperative behaviour as the norm; considers management of oneself the starting point for managing the external world; considers sacrifice of the ego and the following of *dharma* the way in which peace and concord can be attained. The system lays as much stress on individual self-fulfilment as optimization of the organizational objectives and, in fact, considers the two to be inextricably linked together like the reverse and obverse of a coin. The way to achieving this harmony between the internal and the external, the worlds of spirit and matter, is through the following of *dharma* and *rita*, the universal order. The Vedic management system, thus, has to be *dharmic* in its methodology. The details of how it operates in the social and political spheres is dealt with later.

REFERENCES

1. Swami Sri Bharati Krishna Trithaji Maharaj, *Vedic Mathematics* (Delhi: Motilal Banarasidas, 1988).
2. Vannucchi, M. *Ecological Readings in the Veda* (Delhi: D.K. Printworld (P) Ltd., 1994).
3. David Frawley, *Gods, Sages and Kings*, (Delhi: Motilal Banarasidass, 1995).
4. Sri Aurobindo, *The Secret of the Veda*, (Pondicherry: Sri Aurobindo Ashram, 1971).
5. The five sense organs are the eyes, ears, nose, taste-buds and skin receptors.
6. Brahman is the name given to the Impersonal God.
7. Kena Upanishad, 1.3.
8. Taittiriya Upanishad, 2.1.4.
9. Shvetasvatara Upanishad, 4.1.
10. *Ibid.*, 3.3.
11. Rig Veda, 10.90.1. The word *purusha* means man; here it means the original principle of Consiciousness.
12. Rig Veda, 10.90.3, 4.
13. See Rig Veda, 10.164.46 which says "the One is called Mitra, Varuna, Yama and Matarishvan".
14. *Bhagavad Gita*, 15.1, 2. The *gunas* are the three qualities

in the world of form: harmony (*sattva*), action (*rajas*) and inertia (*tamas*).

15. Rig Veda, 10.81: 82.
16. Chhandogya Upanishad, 3,19.1.
17. e.g., Rig Veda, 10.129.3, Prashna Upanishad, 1.4.
18. cf. *Bhagvad Gita*, 3.10, which says, "Thus spoke the Lord of creation when he made both man and sacrifice: 'By sacrifice thou shalt multiply and obtain all thy desires?
19. Rig Veda, 10.90.8-15.
20. According to Panikkar the root of *rita* is r-, ar-, to put in motion; the root ar- means to fit, to arrnage (the spokes in the wheel), so that *rita* would be that which is well arranged, the established norm, 'truth,' order, etc., but always with a dynamic connotation. See, Raimundo Panikkar, *The Vedic Experience* (Delhi: Motilal Banarasidas, 1994) p. 350.
21. cf., Rig Veda, which says:

    "From austerity, cosmic order (*rita*) came and truth" (10.190.1).
22. cf., Rig Veda which says:

    "Those Lords of *rita*, of light, I invoke who uphold *rita* by means of *rita*, Mitra and Varuna" (1.23.5).
23. cf., Rig Veda, 4.23.9.
24. Atharva Veda, 12.1.17 which speaks of the earth "as upheld by Dharman".
25. Rig Veda, 8.70.11.
26. "This dejection is un-Aryan, unbecoming, infamous. O Arjuna"—*Bhagavad Gita*, 2.2.
27. Atharva Veda, 12.2.26.
28. Rig Veda, 8.5.1.9.
29. Rig Veda, 5.85.7
30. Rig Veda, 10.90.12.
31. Atharva Veda, 4.16.8.
32. "Strengthen knowledge, strengthen valour"—Yajur Veda, 6.3.
33. Yajur Veda, 20.25.
34. Yajur Veda, 18.48.

35. Aitareya Upanishad, peace chant as a prelude to the teaching.

36. Smriti means to remember. Indian tradition is divided into *shruti*, or scripture that has been 'heard' in a spiritual audience, and *smriti* which tries to develop the *shruti* into logically formulated rules and laws.

37. Bhagavad Gita. 18.66.

38. Swadharma means *dharma* flowing from a persons nature and place in the societal structure.

39. *Laws of Manu*, 1886 tr. by G. Buhler, reprinted 1982, Delhi: Motilal Banarsidas, 12.88. In later citations the laws of Manu will be referred to by the word Manu.

40. Rig Veda, 8.41.3.

41. Rig Veda, 10.148.4.

42. Atharva Veda, 19.15.4-6.

43. Brihadaranayaka Upanishad, 4.2.4.

44. Katha Upanishad, 2.11

45. *Ibid.*, 1.12.

46. Rig Veda, 10.68.1.

47. Translated and quoted in *Hindu Spirituality*, K. Sivaraman (ed.) (Delhi: Motilal Banarsidas, 1995) p. 3.

48. For example, Rig Veda, translated by Ralph T.H. Griffith (London: 1889 reprinted Delhi: Motilal Banarsidas, 1973) which says:

    What is the One who in the form of the unborn propped apart these six realms of space (1.164.6).

    The One of whom the wise speak of variously (1.164.46).

49. See, for example, Fritjof Capra, *The Tao of Physics* (New York: Fontana Books, 1976).

3

THE PSYCHOLOGICAL APPROACH OF THE UPANISHADS

There is a general tendency to regard the Upanishadic thought as dealing with the internal aspects of man while the Vedas deal with the external. In fact, the Upanishads are only a culmination of Vedic thought. They continue to use the synthesizing methodology developed in the Vedas including the stress that the Vedic seers laid on retaining names and forms while at the same time, where necessary, changing the inner and spiritual content. The Upanishads also carry further the process initiated by the Vedas of harmonizing and reconciling everything, including that which seems at first sight to be seemingly irreconcilable. They state more explicitly and openly the mysticism that in the Vedas is veiled by somewhat obscure language capable of being understood only by the adepts and practitioners.

The Upanishads base themselves on the system developed by the intuitive minds and intimate psychological experiences of the Vedic seers. 'The Upanishads are the essence of the Vedas', says the Upanishad, 'and the Divine is the source of the Vedas'[1]. The Kena Upanishad says (4.8) that the Vedas are the limbs of the Upanishads:

> Concentration of thought, self-control and action are the foundations of the Upanishad, the Vedas are all its limbs, while truth is its abode.

The imagery used by the Upanishads is also in large measure developed from the type of imagery found in the Vedas. There are a number of passages in the Upanishads that take up the fundamental ideas of the Vedic mind and temperament and develop them in the light of a more open and advanced spirituality. A comparison of the following passage from the Katha Upanishad with a similar verse from the Rig Veda which speaks of the 'baseless region where King Varuna of hallowed power, holds erect the tree's stem; its rays, whose root is high above, stream downward; may they sink within us and be hidden'[2], would illustrate the point:

> This is the ancient Ashvattha tree whose roots are above and whose branches spread below.
>
> That is verily the pure, that is Brahman, and that is also called immortal.
>
> In that rest all the worlds and none can transcend it. Verily this is that[3].

As is apparent, the Upanishad uses the imagery of the tree in a spiritually more open fashion to explain the involution of the Divine into the universe of name and form. It has grafted its own ideas of Brahman and the Immortal on to the imagery of the Rig Veda. This is in line with the Vedic methodology, continued by the Upanishads, of transforming inner content while leaving unchanged the outer form. The Upanishad also replaces Varuna, the god mentioned in the Rig Veda, by the Brahman, and while Varuna only holds aloft the tree, the Brahman, the pure, is the tree, and all that exists, and whom none can transcend.

The Upanishads, thus, are not a revolutionary departure from the Vedas but a continuation and a development, and to a certain extent an enlarging transfomation in the sense of bringing into open expression all that was held covered by the symbolic Vedic speech as a mystery and a secret. The manner in which the Upanishads take up the imagery and ritual symbols of the Vedas and thereafter transform the outward symbols by bringing out their inner and mystic sense to serve as the starting point for their more highly evolved and spiritual philosophy can be seen from the following passage from the Isha Upanishad. This is based on a Vedic verse which speaks of that which is 'hidden by your truth but (which) is the Truth that is constant for ever (and) where they unyoke the horses of the Sun; there the thousands of his rays come together, there is the one: I have seen the Supreme Godhead of the gods'[4]. The Isha Upanishad (15, 16) says:

> Like a golden lid the shining orb covers the entrance to the Truth in Thee. Remove it O Sun, so that I who am devoted to the True may behold that. O Sun, lonely courser of heaven, O Yama, O son of Prajapati contract Thy rays, withdraw thy light. Through Thy grace, I behold the most blessed form of Thine. I am indeed He, that Being who dwells there.

The change in the spiritual content of the latter of the two passages is evident. Though in both passages the Sun is involved as the godhead of knowledge and light and is requested to contract his rays whereby his supreme effulgence and truth may become visible (and knowledge become one-pointed instead of being widely diffused). The Upanishad also adds that the Being there and here is the same, thereby taking the perception of divinity to a sublime and superior level. Thus, though the imagery and style of the Upanishad is akin to that of the Veda, the Upanishad translates into a more open assertion the unity between the macrocosm and the microcosm, the divine and the human, and states clearly that which is secret, symbolic and hidden in the Veda.

The manner in which the thought of the Upanishads transforms the concrete imagery of the Vedas, even at its highest philosophical level, into diction which reveals its inner spiritual content in a magnificently open and sublime imagery can be seen from the two passages cited below, one being from the Rig Veda and the other being from the Taittiriya Upanishad.

> There was neither non-reality nor reality then;

There was no air nor sky which is beyond it.
What covered it and where? Whose was the shelter?
Was water there, fathomless and deep?
Death then existed not, nor immortality,
Neither of day nor of night was there any sign;
The One breathed, airless, by self-impulse,
Apart from It was nothing whatsoever.

Rig Veda, 10.129.1,2.

In the beginning all this Universe was nonexistent and unmanifest, from which this manifest existence was born. Itself created itself; none other created it. Therefore they say of it the well and beautifully made. So, this that is well and beautifully made, verily it is the delight behind existence. When he hath gotten him this delight, then it became a thing of bliss; for who could breathe, who remain alive, if this Bliss were not in the ether.

Taittiriya Upanishad, 2.7.

It is obvious that the two self-created entities are the same, the original cause, the creator of the universe. The Vedic one breathes by self-impulse, the other also by self-impulse but in the ether of bliss. The illumined Upanishadic experience of a revelatory and intuitive mind brings at once before the soul's eye a suggestive thought that discovers a whole infinite through a seemingly finite image. From the nothing or the vacuum of the Vedic thought we come to the bliss, the *ananda*, of the Upanishads, to the delight behind existence. The end to be is joy and bliss and not a nothingness.

The Upanishads also address prayers to the Vedic gods. The Aiteraya Upanishad pleads for 'the Vedic lore not to forsake the aspirant so that he may join night and day and always think and speak the truth'[5]. In the first chapter of the Mahanarayana Upanishad a large number of verses are addressed to Vedic gods and goddesses like Indra, Durga, Agni, the Earth, etc., praying for earthly prosperity, well-being, sons, destruction of enemies, etc.[6] The

Brihadaranayaka Upanishad, expounding the science of the infinite, towards the very end, reproduces a large number of verses intended to help the worshipper get good sons and greatness in the world.[7] The Shwetashvatara Upanishad prays to Rudra for 'protection with his benevolent face' and 'not to injure children, grandchildren, cows and horses', and also 'not to destroy our heroes'[8]

It is not only for earthly favours that the Upanishads appeal to the Vedic gods but also for intellectual strength which, in the Upanishadic scheme of things, is one of the prime instruments necessary for the realisation of the Divine. 'May Indra increase intellect unto me for my strengthening', says the Taittiriya, 'O God may I become a vessel of immortality'[9]. Another Upanishad goes on to say:

> O Rudra, who blesses all creatures by revealing the Vedas, deign to make us happy by Thy calm and blissful self which roots out terror as well as sin.[10]

The Upanishads accept the efficacy of the Vedic hymns for taking the evolving soul to higher and meritorious worlds after death. 'Whatever ritualistic works the sages have created elaborately in the three Vedas are true. Ye lovers of the truth, perform them constantly, for they are to you the paths to the world of meritorious deeds'.[11] But the way of sacrifices, of the Vedic ritual is said to be the lower knowledge for it leads not to the eternal. 'Verily frail are the ships of sacrifices, frail these forms of sacrifice, all eighteen of them, on which rests the inferior work devoid of knowledge'.[12] Those who attach themselves only to the lower kind of action, go round and round like the blind led by the blind, and being subject to attachment.

> Those deluded men fancying sacrifices as the highest, fall into human birth, or even lower still, after reaping the fruits of their virtuous deeds in the highest heavens.[13]

The Upanishadic Concept of Man

Since they did not see Vedic rituals as leading to the highest attainment, the Upanishadic seers directed their attention to both the external world as well as to the internal world of man. Their study convinced them that an exclusive concentration on the external universe would not help in solving the problem of the ultimate Reality which had, in any case, to be conceived of and understood by the human consciousness. They discovered that the inner world of man, including the mind and its modifications, was an extremely complex entity which was in its own way, as mysterious, interesting and complicated, as was the outer world.

According to the Upanishadic concept, the subsystem of man is composed of both the gross and the subtle. Its substratum is the same divine conciousness that pervades the universe and its evolution from the gross to the subtle is the way by which the eternal can be realized. Once the human soul is seized by this compelling desire for the ultimate reality, it is no longer satisfied with looking upon the world of forms and constant change through those doors of the mind and senses which the Self-existent has made to open outward; but rather it is driven to gaze inward into a new world of realities.[14]

The senses and the sense-objects, belonging to name and form, are within the space-time continuum and subject to causation. The Upanishads hold that the ultimate reality, being beyond name and form, cannot be comprehended or understood by that which is finite and subject to the dualities of the manifested universe. 'That Atman', says the Upanishad, 'can never be reached by speech nor by the eyes nor even the mind'[15].

The Eternal, which is of the nature of the infinite, is thus inconceivable and indefinable by finite and defining mind, just as it is inexpressible by mind-created speech. Attainment of the eternal, says the Upanishad, leads to the cessation of all regrets and all desires.

> The bliss of the eternal is that from which words turn back without attaining and the mind also returneth baffled. He who knoweth the bliss of the eternal, verily to him cometh not remorse or torment at not having done the right or having done wrong; for he knoweth

them both and delivereth his spirit from them on knowing the eternal.[16]

Here we reach the One who is not the Vedic unified existence whom the sages call by various names but is the absolute Brahman referred to in the neuter gender as the That. The result is that the Upanishadic gods, become unaware of their divine origins so that even the chief gods, Vayu, Agni and Indra are unable to understand and comprehend the power and might of Brahman.[17] Though the Rig Veda had referred to the God 'to whom all gods paid worship'[18] as well as to 'the God above all gods'[19] nowhere in the Veda had the transcendental absolute become what he was to become in the Upanishads: The One both immanent in, and transcending the universe, and while being devoid of all qualities and characteristics yet having them all in the absolute and eternal sense.

The Upanishads also made the various Vedic deities the powers of consciousness in addition to their being the powers of nature. They correlated the different deities with the various senses following a hint to this effect in the Atharva Veda which speaks of 'the gods entering into him after they had fused the mortal man complete' and of how 'man is regarded as this Brahman for verily all deities abide in him as cows in a pen'[20]. An Upanishad declares that the Self or Spirit after deciding to create, first created the different worlds, and then their guardians or the gods. Feeling hunger and thirst they, the gods, asked the Spirit for a place where they could establish themselves and eat food.[21] The Spirit first formed animal kinds like the cow and the horse, but the gods found them to be insufficient vehicles; and so the Spirit finally created the form of man which the gods found to be excellently made and sufficient, and they entered into it for the performance of their functions. Agni entered the organ of speech, the Sun the eyes, Vayu the nostrils, the deities of the quarters the ears, the deities of herbs and trees the skin, and the moon the mind.[22] In another passage, the Taittiriya Upanishad (1.4) clearly declares Indra as the power and godhead of the purified and intuitive mind.

> He who is the bull of the Vedas of the universal form, he who was born in the sacred rhythms from the Immortal, may Indra increase my intellect. O God, may I become a vessel of the Immortal. My body be full of vision and my tongue of sweetness, may I hear the much and vast with my ears. For thou art the sheath of Brahman covered over and hidden by the intelligence.

The Upanishads then go on to establish the relationship between the gods and Brahman. In the external world we have already seen how in the Kena Upanishad it is said that even the chief gods, including Indra, the godhead of the intelligence, could not get to know and to comprehend Brahman. The Brihadaranayaka Upanishad goes on to say that even the gods cannot prevail against the man who has realized Brahman, since he becomes their very self. But he who worships a god thinking him as different from oneself, becomes as an animal to the gods, serving the gods in the same way as animals serve man.[23] The Upanished goes on to assert that the performance of sacrifices, or *yagya*, to someone regarded as different from oneself makes a person a servant of the gods.[24] While recognizing the efficacy of the Vedas and accepting that the Vedas are projected by the Infinite together with sacrifices, spiritual practices and all that the Vedas declare[25], the Upanishads in the freedom of their thought go beyond the Vedas.

> After studying the Vedas the intelligent one who is solely intent in acquiring knowledge and realization, should discard the Vedas altogether, as the man who seeks to obtain rice discards the husk.[26]

The approach of the Upanishads to the Vedic thought and system is, thus, not one of rejection, but rather an acceptance of all that the Vedas stand for, whether in their concept of the gods, sacrifices or rituals. Accepting, as the Upanishadic seers did, the presence of graded capabilities in different human beings, all that they do is to place the matter in perspective by delineating the differential results that flow from different kinds of behaviour and actions. Thereafter they leave it to each individual to follow the path considered most suitable by him. And as we shall see later on, the concepts get more and more subtle as the delineation of the Upanishadic system progresses.

The Upanishads also address themselves to the question of harmonising the internal and the external, that is, the subjective and inner world of man with the objective universe. Their approach is that, whatever there is in the external is also in the internal. The gods thus become both the powers of nature and of consciousness thereby unifying the external with the internal. The Upanishads also speak of the processes of involution and evolution, with the Divine coming into nature through the process of involution and man rising out of nature through the process of evolution. Both during the processes of involution and evolution, the milestones to be passed on the way are the same, namely, matter, energy, mind, intuitive thought and bliss for the evolving soul, etc., downwards to matter for the Divine in its process of involution.[27] As we shall see later on, in the Upanishadic scheme all the external powers are controlled by Brahman, and the inner ones by the Atman, the inner controller. The harmonization and unification is completed by the Upanishadic declaration of the identity of the Brahman with the Atman.

The Vedic attitude to life and nature was positive and activist making the Vedas to apparently put a somewhat greater stress on the external in contrast to that put on the internal. The Upanishads set out to redress the balance and re-establish harmony between the external and the internal by stressing the necessity of an inward turning of the mind and consciousness.

> The self-born has set the doors of the body to face outwards, therefore the soul of a man gazes outward and not at the Self within; hardly a wise man here and there, desiring immortality, turns his eyes inward and sees the Self within him.[28]

The Mahanarayana Upanishad carries the matter further. Stating that there are various opinions being held as to what are the means of liberation, it goes on to say that the practise of truthfulness, austerity, withdrawal of senses from forbidden objects, giving of selfless gifts, scriptural duty and procreation (the son being the way to the land of the ancestors, *pitriloka*) are all very difficult to practise and are conducive to the highest good. Those devoted to the Vedic religion stress *agnihotre* and *yagya* and these also lead to the highest good. The wise, however, consider inward worship as the means of liberation with complete renunciation and dispassion, *sannyasa*, as surpassing all the austerities mentioned earlier and therefore being considered the supreme remedy.[29] The same succession of activities are again repeated in the Mahanarayana Upanishad in the form of a dialogue between Prajapati and his son Aruni where speaking of inward worship, renunciation and dispassion, it is said 'inward worship is the means of attaining the state of Prajapati and is therefore referred to as the supreme means of liberation... (while)... wise seers aver that *sannyasa*, mentioned as the supreme means of liberation, is Brahman, the Universal Spirit'[30].

As we have noted the Vedas speak of poets and seers who either imagine or conceive of the One in different ways. The Upanishads, which are post-Vedic, adopt the same liberal attitude. The oneness of the Supreme is insisted on, but variety of description is permitted. The light of absolute truth is said to be refracted as it passes through the imperfect human mind. In the boundless being of the One are all the powers that are worshipped as gods, not as it they were standing side by side in space, but each a facet mirroring the whole, or a hologram if we were to say it in modern language.

Buddha relates the story of a certain king of Benares in the ancient past who desiring to divert himself, gathered together a number of beggars blind from birth and offered a prize to the one who should give him the best account of an elephant. The first beggar who examined the elephant chanced to lay hold of the leg, and reported that an elephant was like a tree-trunk; the second, laying hold of the tail, declared that an elephant was like a rope; another, who seized an ear, insisted that an elephant was like a palm-leaf; and so on. The beggars started quarrelling with one another and the king was greatly amused. The moral of the story is: ordinary teachers who have grasped this or that aspect of the truth quarrel with one another, while only a Buddha knows the whole. In theological discussions we are at best blind beggars fighting with one another. The complete vision is difficult to attain since Buddhas are rare.

In the above story those who are 'blind' to the reality cannot grasp it; it requires the 'opening' of the eyes for them to have the holistic vision. Sri Krishna tells Arjuna in the *Bhagavad Gita* (11.8):

> But thou never can'st see Me with these thy mortal eyes: I will give thee divine sight.

It was only when his eyes had been 'opened' (the so called Third Eye referred to in many mystical traditions) that Arjuna could exclaim:

> I see in thee all the gods, O my God; and the infinity of the beings of thy creation... All around I behold thy Infinity: The power of thy innumerable arms, the visions from thy innumerable eyes, the words from thy innumerable mouths. Nowhere do I see Thy beginning or middle or end.[31]

God and Man

For further elucidating the relations between God and man, the Upanishads delineate two subsystems. One subsystem describes the relations of the divine with the universe including the involution, or the descent, of the divine into the world. The other subsystem explores the inner world of man.

The divine is held to transcend the world while being simultaneously immanent in it. The divine also is said to pervade everything in the universe and 'He is the entire universe; earth and sky, the mind and the life—breaths are all woven into Him'[32]. He is static as well as dynamic, the energyless as well as the unceasing fountain of strength, power and will. He projects energy in order to create the universe. The universe springs from Him, rests and moves in Him and in the end merges in Him.

> As the spider draws its thread out of itself, as shrubs and plants grow from the earth, as the hair grows on the bodies of persons, so has all this universe come out of the imperishable.[33]

In this transcendental aspect, the divine is viewed as the sole absolute or the ultimate reality. He is considered to be beyond all dualities, beyond space—time and causation, beyond birth and death. He is the one without a second[34], the unchangeable in all changes and the indivisible in the midst of all divisions. He projects the universe after entering into it.

> He, the origin and dissolution of the universe, is seated in one's own self and is perceived as different from and transcending, the tree of the world as well as time and form.[35]

The other subsystem, that of the inner world of man, is delineated by the Upanishads into the gross, the subtle and the causal bodies and the five sheaths with the finer ones permeating the grosser formations. The material sheath and the sheath of life form the gross body, the mental sheath forms the subtle body, and the knowledge sheath and the sheath of bliss form the causal body. The most subtle of all, and which therefore pervades them all, is the Atman or the Self.

> There is a self that is of the essence of matter–there is another inner self of life that fills the other–there is another inner self of mind–there is another inner self of knowledge–there is another inner self of bliss.[36]

But the Atman is, in its essence, no different from the Brahman. It is the Brahman which has entered the body of man and as the inner self and the internal ruler, presides over and guides all actions.

> God, who is the only One, is hidden in all beings. He is all-pervading, and is the inner self of all creatures.

> He presides over all actions, and all beings reside in Him.[37]
>
> He who inhabits all beings, but is within them, whom no being knows, whose body is all beings, and who controls all beings from within, is the internal ruler, your own immortal self... who controls this and the next life and all beings from within.[38]

The same essential consciousness is thus both immanent in nature and transcends it. It transcends the universe as Being and is immanent in the universe as the power of Being. 'Know then that nature is Maya', says the Upanishad, 'and the great God is the Lord of Maya. The whole world is filled with beings who form His parts'[39]. The Atman in the body is of the essence of consciousness[40], and is of the size of a thumb and dwells within the body. It is the Lord of the past and the future and is the same as Brahman. This realization is what takes the soul beyond death to immortality.

> The Purusha of the size of a thumb dwells within the body. He is the lord of the past and the future.
>
> Whatever is here, that is there; what is there, the same is here. From death to death he goes who sees different.[41]

Though the substratum of the two subsystems, of god and the universe and of man, is essentially the same, yet the relations between the two subsystems are of a very complex nature. The perception of the universe has to be through the various levels and planes of the human consciousness. Since the senses and the mind have to function through these different levels or planes of consciousness, the perception of the cosmos, as it is normally cognized, tends to make cosmic existence appear an indeterminate, if not an indeterminable entity. Relations with the ultimate also tend to be incapable of pragmatic or empirical relationship though the ultimate has to be known if the transient and ever-changing universe has to be transcended and immortality achieved.

The unseen with whom there can be no pragmatic

> relations, unseizable, featureless, unthinkable, undesignable by name, whose substance is the certitude of One self, in whom world existence is settled, who is all peace and bliss—that is the self, that is what must be known.[42]

The complexity is further heightened by the fact that the universe, too, is composed of the gross, the subtle and the causal. The different worlds, or *lokas*, conceived of by the Vedas, and later on modified by the Upanishads, are, in their essence, gross. The worlds are produced by the five gross elements (the *mahabhutas*), namely, ether, air, fire, water, earth, and these very elements produce the four kinds of gross bodies dwelling therein and the food and drink appropriate to them. The four gross bodies are (i) those born of the womb like man and various animals; (ii) those born of eggs, like birds and reptiles; (iii) those born of moisture, like mosquitoes and lice, and (iv) those that are born of earth, like trees and creepers. The five gross elements, unlike the five subtle elements which are rudimentary (*tanmatra*) and mixed, are in the nature of compounds. Each gross element consists of one half portion of its subtle counterpart and one eighth of each of the four remaining subtle elements. Though consisting of all subtle elements, the characteristic (sound, touch, etc.) of each gross element is based on its preponderant subtle element.

The symmetrical nature of the two subsystems in which each subsystem is composed of the causal, the subtle and the gross is further emphasized by the Upanishadic concept of the universe also being composed of matter, life-energy, mind, knowledge and bliss. The higher planes of the universe corresponding to the above categories are conceived to be of increasing degrees of refinement and so can only be perceived if human consciousness is made subtler and subtler through concentration of thought or *tapas*.

> Varuna's son, Bhrigu, asked his father to instruct him about Brahman. His father declared to him 'matter, life-energy, sight, hearing, mind and speech—even

these. Seek to know through *tapas* that from which all beings are born, whereby being born they live, and to which they go and enter again; for that is Brahman.'

He concentrated in thought and understood matter to be Brahman... he concentrated further and understood life-energy as Brahman... he concentrated again and understood mind to be Brahman... he concentrated again and understood knowledge to be Brahman... further concentration revealed bliss to be Brahman.[43]

The two subsystems are thus mirror images of each other in the sense of being capable of being divided into the gross, the subtle and the causal, and also because they are both composed of matter which is successively permeated by life-energy, mind, knowledge and bliss. The subtler elements of both the subsystems converge towards pure consciousness and in fact the subtlest essence of both is, respectively, Brahman and Atman. However, the very similarity of the two subsystems makes for differential perceptions of the universe. Since each individual is capable of refining his consciousness to as subtle a plane as he wants to, and is prepared to work for, there is a complex interplay of forces and perceptions in which the universe is subjectively perceived by each individual to be different from what others perceive it to be. Furthermore, even the same individual would perceive the universe differently at different times depending on the state of his consciousness at that particular moment. This concept makes each individual, and his perceptions unique.

One further point needs to be noted at this stage. The cosmology of the Upanishads may appear crude, as far as details are concerned, in the light of the discoveries of modern science. But its relativistic and indeterminate character is, in principle, in harmony with the modern scientific theories of relativity and indeterminacy. Besides it has to be borne in mind that to the Upanishadic seers the purpose of establishing a cosmology was not to explain the universe and its origin, but to establish, through it, the ultimate reality of Brahman. For to them the universe, divorced from Brahman, was unimportant from the standpoint of value. Their intention was, therefore, not to analyse the nature of the universe but though the cosmology developed by them of facilitate the realization of Brahman. And to this end, as we shall see later, they laid down subjectively verifiable criteria. The approach of laying down a theory or hypothesis capable of experimental verification is, in fact, scientific to the highest degree.

The Upanishadic System

In spite of structural similarities, and the fact of the substratum of the two subsystems being the same in essence, there are difficulties in the path of realization of this essential unity. One reason for this is the difference in the relations of Maya, or Prakriti, with God and man. Whereas Prakriti, or Maya, is the 'inscrutable power of the Lord' who, through Maya, projects all the worlds, Vedas and beings, in the case of man, Maya acts as a veiling power on his consciousness and perceptions thereby making difficult for him the realization of the truth.

> The One assumes manifold powers and appears the Divine Lord by virtue of His inscrutable power of Maya.[44]

> The individual grieves because he is not the Lord... sacrifices and ritual and vows, what has been and what is to be, and what the Vedas declare, and the whole world are projected by the Lord of Maya in all this.[45]

The Upanishads also distinguish between the soul and God by referring to the individual soul, the *jiva*, like unto the sparks of a blazing fire which though having a common source, appear as different. The soul and God are also spoken of as like unto two birds on the tree of nature; and while one bird (the human soul) eats and enjoys the fruits of the tree, the other does not. They are also referred to as the two in this world whom the knowers of the Brahman refer to as the light and the shade. All sorrow passes away, the Upanishads say, when the individual soul realizes his identity with the divine.

> This is That, the Truth of things: as from one high

> kindled fire thousands of different sparks are born and all have the same form of fire, so, O fair son, from the immutable manifold becomings are born and even into that they depart.[46]

Because of the non-realisation of its identity with the immutable the individual soul goes from death to death or, to look at it in another way, from birth to birth, or becoming to becoming. He goes to the different worlds depending on his deeds and the level of consciousness he has attained here in the body. The deities, or gods, who are the guardians of the different worlds, are also simultaneously the Lords of consciousness. So depending on his deeds, and the stage of consciousness that he attains to, the individual soul goes to the appropriate higher or lower world. The connecting links in this process of transmigration are the gods, who in addition to being the guardians of the different worlds are the powers of consciousness and of nature.

> The spirit thought, 'Lo, there are the worlds; and now will I make me guardians for my worlds'[47].

The attainment of the highest stage of consciousness has to be here in the body, in this very world and not in some paradise or heaven. According to what a man meditates on, is his attainment of worlds after death, and only meditation on the Supreme Eternal leads to the highest world of light and energy.

> If one is unable to realize here, before the fall of the body, one has to take body again in the worlds of creation.[48]

> Meditation on one letter of OM leads the soul to attainment of the material universe and the world of men; meditation on the second leads to the lunar world where he experiences greatness; and meditation on all the three letters take him to the solar world of light and energy.[49]

The theory of transmigration of the soul as enunciated by the Upanishads suggests some other links between the two subsystems. These links are of a dynamic nature since they either lead to fresh becomings or births, or help in working out the impact of whatever has been done in the past. The links are dynamic since they serve to move the soul of man from one world of existence to another, or from one birth to another birth. These links between man and the divine take place in nature, or the universe, and so are under the control of Maya.

The links can be activated both by the Divine and by man. But being pragmatic thinkers, the Vedic seers concentrated more on what man could do since that was something within the reach and control of the individual himself. But it is through Divine grace that the soul attains to the Eternal and becomes free; and it is He who as the inner controller, guides the individual. This He does not do in an arbitrary manner but according to tendencies evolved in previous births, and according to karma, the actions of individuals, He decrees the appropriate fruit or result.

> He makes those whom He will raise do good deeds.[50]

> He controls all beings from within.[51]

The grace of the Divine has to be won by the actions of the individual. Actions, though guided by the Divine, flow from past actions and tendencies which act as the constraints through which the Divine guides the mind and actions of the individual. But the Upanishads stress the grace of the Divine as absolutely essential. According to them however hard the individual may strive, it is in the ultimate analysis a descent of the Divine that takes place and whereby He discloses Himself to the individual.

> The Self is not to be won by eloquent teaching, nor by brain power, nor by much learning; but only he whom this Being chooses can win Him, for to him this Self bares His body.[52]

> Subtler than even the subtlest and greater than the greatest, the Atman is concealed in the heart of creatures. By the grace of the Creator, one becomes free from sorrows and desires, and then realizes Him as the great Lord.[53]

The grace of the divine is to be obtained through devotion and austerity. *Tapas*, concentration in thought and actions, is given a very high place in the Upanishadic scheme of things. Concentration has a two-way link with purity: Through concentration purity does its works, while purity is the necessary condition in which concentration becomes entire and effective. Concentration means the gathering back of thought into itself and through this action a great holiness, purity and peace descends on the individual. In the end, the cessation of all turbulent thought leads to an ascent to the absolute and transcendent stage whereby the individual attains the heaven of the spirit. This is illustrated by the story of Bhrigu who through the practice of *tapas* went from subtler to subtler forms till he reached the state of bliss and 'understood that bliss was Brahman; for certainly all beings here are, indeed, born from bliss; having been born, they remain alive by bliss; and on departing, they enter into bliss'[54]. *Tapas* also it was, what the Creator underwent for projecting the universe; He brooded on Himself and the entire universe of name and form came forth.[55] The Upanishads give *tapas* pride of place in the actions necessary for man to be able to overcome all obstacles and thereafter realize Brahman. It is both a precondition and a stage to be gone through before knowledge can be disclosed by the realized ones to the aspirant who desires to know the path to the ultimate.

> The Rishi said to them: 'Another year ye dwell in holiness and faith and *tapas*: then ask what ye will, and if I know, surely I will conceal nothing'[56].

> Practise truth, *rita*, *tapas* and self-restraint along with study and meditation on the Vedas.... the various sages held *tapas*, truthfulness, and study and imparting of the Vedas as sufficient. That assuredly is *tapas*.[57]

In the Upanishadic scheme, truth is another important category. The main characteristics of Brahman are stated to be truth, knowledge and infinity and the realization of that is said to lead to the highest heaven. Yet in the world of duality even absolute truth becomes relative and has within itself varying degrees of untruth. Only by constantly practising truth and purifying the senses, mind, etc. can the truth be realized. Truth is lauded at many places in the Upanishads as a critical instrumentality for the realization of the Ultimate.

> Truth is Brahman... in the middle is untruth which is enclosed on either side by truth. There is thus a preponderance of truth.[58]

Not only is truth a critical instrumentality in the search for the Divine, but it is only through truth, say the Upanishads, that the self can be won. *Dharma*, righteousness, is considered synonymous with truth. Both *dharma*, the truth, along with the learning of the Vedas, have to be followed by the disciple; for the practice of *dharma* and truth are declared to be indispensable in the quest for the Divine.

> Righteousness (*dharma*) is superior to everything and there is nothing higher than it. That righteousness is verily truth, and truth is but righteousness.[59]

The objects of desire all flow from knowledge and actions in the world. The Upanishads while recognizing the efficacy of Vedic hymns or *mantras* and *yagyas* or sacrifice as leading to superior planes of existence at the same time divide knowledge into two aspects, the higher and the lower. While the lower knowledge leads to the worlds of meritorious deeds, only the higher leads to the imperishable.

> The ritualistic works found in the mantras, and treated elaborately in the Vedas, are true... they lead to the world of meritorious deeds.[60]

> There is a lower and a higher knowledge. Lower knowledge consists of study of the Vedas, phonetics, code of rituals, grammar, etymology, metrics and astronomy. By the higher, the imperishable is attained. That which is invisible, ungraspable, unoriginated and attributeless, it has neither eyes, nor ears, nor hands, nor feet; It is eternal all pervading, immeasurably subtle and limitless.[61]

The Vedic concept of sacrifice is also further developed and elaborated by the Upanishads. The Upanishads declare that a human being, unlike animals, is not a mere instrument of his instincts. He can discriminate between right and wrong, true and false, noble and ignoble, good and pleasant. The instinctive urges are no doubt strong in man; but guided by reason, he can develop will power to control the natural impulses and pursue his chosen course. He has the power of decision as well as the choice of action. He can dominate and direct the lower self by the higher self. This self-mastery constitutes the real nature of man. Man's advancement, according to the Upanishads, is proportionate to the development of this virtue. As Sri Krishna says to Arjuna:

> Conquer the lower self by the higher self... (for) only when one has controlled one's (lower) self that one attains to the calmness of self-mastery.[62]

Also in man, self-conciousness is much more developed than in other living beings. He is fully aware of himself as an individual distinct from the rest of the world. He can analyze his own being. He can distinguish the body from the mind, and knows that he has an outer as well as an inner life. He finds that his inner life is greater, deeper, and more glorious than the outer life. The physical body, however dominant and fascinating, forms but the exterior of his personality. The intellectual, moral, aesthetic, and spiritual aspects of life are the expressions of his inner consciousness.

The crowning glory of human life is self-knowledge. Man can know himself as he really is. The body does not constitute his real self, nor the mind, nor the combination of the body and the mind. His real self, the very basis of his ego, is the One who has entered into everything. It is the One that is the knower of the body as well as of the mind. The mind cannot be the knower, because the mind is known. There is something beyond that which watches the mind. The mind falls into the category of the object. It should not be identified with the subject, the knower. The self-intelligent One which watches all physical and mental events, is the only invariable factor in the human personality.

Such is the self of man. But through mysterious ignorance he gets identified with the body and the mind and ascribes to himself all that belong to them. Thus, the unconditioned spirit becomes subject to all physical and mental conditions. As soon as man can realize his distinctness from the psychophysical adjuncts and his oneness with the Supreme Being, he becomes free from all bondages. The attainment of this freedom is the highest goal of life. One can attain it even while living in the body. It is the ignorance of the true nature of the self which is the prime cause of bondage, and not the body nor the mind.

There have been great seers and saints in different climes and ages who have realized this freedom and proclaimed it to be the supreme end of life. So declares the Upanishadic seer, "I have realized this self-effulgent supreme being beyond darkness. By knowing Him alone one overcomes mortality. There is no other way out."[63] He who knows the truth, becomes one with the truth, because the truth is his very self. You cannot objectify your own self. You simply recognize the self. "The knower of Brahman becomes Brahman (the supreme being)," says the Mundaka Upanishad (3.2.9). Why? Because "That thou art."[64]

The great Chinese sage Lao Tzu, in the sixth century BC, spoke in a similar strain:

> Without going outside one's door, one understands (all that takes place) under the sky; without looking out from one's window, one sees the Tao of heaven. The farther one goes out (from oneself), the less one knows.
>
> Therefore the sages got their knowledge without travelling; gave the (right) names to things without seeing them and accomplished their ends without any purpose of doing so.[65]

The Yogic Way

The Upanishads, thus, conceive of multiple links between man, the universe and the divine. In the static sense, the subsystem of God and the universe, and that of man and his inner world, are structurally conceived as being similar. Their analytical categories are the gross, the subtle and the causal; at the same time the foundation of both the universe and of man is stated to be matter which is successively pervaded by the finer elements of the life-force, mind, knowledge and bliss. The goal of the Vedantic seers was to know the self, to live in it and to be one with it by identity. And through this endeavour they came to see that the self in man is one with the universal self of all things and that this self again is the same as God and Brahman, or transcendent Being or Existence. They also proclaimed that it was possible to behold, live and feel the inmost truth of all things in the universe. According to them the inmost truth of man's inner and outer existence is illumined by the light of this unifying vision and through a process of self-knowledge, world-knowledge and God-knowledge.

But though in the static sense this living in the inmost truth of things seemed to have already been achieved through the symmetry underlying the subsystem of man and the universe, in pragmatic fact this was not the case due to the veiling power of Maya which led to the soul of man identifying itself with the transient rather than with the Eternal. The manner in which the One becomes the many, and the Eternal becomes the transient, is sought to be explained through similes and parables, as well as through a cosmology of the universe. The Upanishads proclaim, however, that no pragmatic relationships between the soul of man and the self of God are possible and that the normal instruments available to the individual are inadequate for the purpose of realizing the Eternal.

Being pragmatists, the Upanishadic seers realized that the relations between man and God would vary from individual to individual depending on the stage of development of the individual's consciousness. So they did not set out to establish the one and only true relationship between man and the Divine. They rather set out to elucidate a whole set of relationships between the two depending on the stage of development of the individual. To those of gross minds, God appeared as gross and to those of subtle minds as subtle; for as the Upanishad says; 'He became all this whatsoever that existeth'[66]. So as man conceived of the Divine, so he found Him. But though accepting that the Divine appears differently to different people, the Upanishads declare that the process of self-identity is achieved only through an enlarging of the human consciousness. So the Upanishads insist that at every level there should be a divinising of the consciousness and the understanding of the ultimate reality behind the conceptions of the human mind which is to be attained.

The Upanishads also elaborate other links between the two subsystems; links that lead to the establishment of dynamic equilibria between man and God. From the side of the Divine there is the concept of divine grace and the guidance He gives as the inner ruler located within the heart of all beings; his guidance being constrained by the acquired and inherited tendencies of the human being. The Upanishadic seers elaborate much more fully what can be done by man to manage the total system (of man and the universe) so that his ultimate objectives can be maximized and the goal reached in the shortest possible time. Some like *tapas*, truth, *yagyas*, etc., have already briefly been mentioned. Reference has also been made to *karma*, devotion and the quest for truth. All these actions subtilize the mind, senses and the entire subsystem of man; and every such subtilization leads to finer and subtler relations of man with the Divine. It is for this reason that these links, or actions, have been referred to as dynamic links between the two subsystems for they continue to change the perceptions that the individual has of God and the universe, and thus of the relations between him and the Divine.

The way from the fragmented human personality to an integrated unity according to the Upanishads is through realization of the innermost self which is identifical with the One. Once the human being has integrated his own personality into a unity, it becomes easy for him to "see all beings in the One and the One in all beings".[67] This is the way of going from the Many to the One by the evolutionary inward path, also called the yogic path as it is, in this way that one can get yoked to the Divine.

The Shwetasvatara Upanishad (2.7-12) gives in some detail the method and results of yogic practice:

> Be devoted to the eternal Brahman. Unite the light within you with the light of Brahman. Thus will the source of ignorance be destroyed, and you will rise above *karma*.
>
> Sit upright, holding the chest, throat, and head erect. Turn the senses and the mind inward to the lotus of the heart. Meditate on Brahman with the help of the syllable OM. Cross the fearful currents of the ocean of worldliness by means of the raft of Brahman—the sacred syllable OM.
>
> With earnest effort hold the senses in check. Controlling the breath, regulate the vital activities. As a charioteer holds back his restive horses, so does a persevering aspirant holds back his mind.
>
> Retire to a solitary place. The place must be protected from the wind and rain, and it must have a smooth, clean floor, free from pebbles and dust. It must not be damp, and it must be free from disturbing noises. It must be pleasing to the eye and quieting to the mind. Seated there, practise meditation and other spiritual exercises.
>
> As you practice meditation, you may see in vision forms resembling snow, crystals, smoke, fire, lightning, fireflies, the sun, the moon. These are signs that you are on your way to the revelation to Brahman.
>
> As you become absorbed in meditation, you will realize that the Self is separate from the body and for this reason will not be affected by disease, old age, or death.

It is interesting to note that along with the stress on meditation the Upanishad also delineates the results of practice. Being pragmatic the Upanishadic seers realized the infinite possibilities for self-deception if there were no confirmatory tests laid down detailing as to what happens when a man has realized the eternal. From the purely physical aspects of what happens to the body, the Upanishads go on to detail the mental and physical changes that take place in the individual's personality. Brightness of body, good health, calmness of mind, clearness of complexion, a beautiful voice, an agreeable odour and scantiness of excretions are preliminary physical signs; flashes of lightning, lustrous and effulgent forms, and forms like snow, smoke, etc., are seen by the mind in meditation; desires vanish from the mind and tranquility is attained; and there is a feeling of complete calm and bliss while all knowledge comes to such as a man, say the Upanishads.

> The first signs of entering into Yoga are lightness of body, health, thirstlessness of mind, clearness of complexion, a beautiful voice, an agreeable odour and scantiness of excretions.[68]
>
> Desires vanish even in this life when one has realized the Atman.[69]
>
> Sages who have attained the self get perfected in soul, non-attached and tranquil.[70]
>
> Through that what is unheard becomes heard, the unthought becomes thought out, and the unknown becomes known.[71]

The Upanishads expect the aspirant to be humble enough to verify all his experiences and knowledge against the laid down tests as well as through the illumination of enlightened souls. His teacher is the guide, in addition to the inner guide in the heart, and with their help and grace the individual is expected to optimise his capabilities for managing the system so that his drive for the immortal is facilitated.

This yogic practice had to be preceded by a purificatory process. At the root of all this lay the original distinction made by the sages between the initiate and the non-initiate, between the one who was fit to receive the secret knowledge and revelation and the one who was too gross to receive the subtle secrets. The Upanishadic sages recognized that the human being needs preparation before he can bear higher knowledge and culture. To prepare the individual was itself a subtle art of education, and the educator himself has to be the one who is not only an initiate but also the accomplished, the *siddha*, the perfected one.

The Upanishads lay stress on proper respect being shown to the preceptor and all other learned people. Works that are not blame-worthy in the eyes of the people, that is, works of general public utility, are to be carried out and righteous and good deeds performed. Gifts are to be given with faith, reverence, humility and fellow feeling and not in a spirit of *noblesse oblige*.

> The preceptor advises the disciple. Let your father, mother, preceptor and the guest be like unto a god to you. Do not be negligent of your works unto the Gods or the ancestors. Do works that are without blame before the people and no others. The deeds that we have done that are good and righteous, practise these as religion and no other. Honour the noble and the learned.[72]

Yagyas or sacrifices also lead to purification of mind while, conversely, a purified mind is necessary for *yagyas* to be successful. 'Where fire is churned out, where air is controlled, where soma juice overflows', says the Upanishad, 'there the mind attains perfection'[73]. A purified mind is also necessary for subtilization of the discriminative intelligence so that the perceptions get finer and finer. It is only through the subtle mind that the self can be realised.

> This secret self in all beings is not apparent, but it is seen by means of the supreme reason, the subtle, by those who have the subtle vision.[74]

The Upanishads place emphasis on the attainment of knowledge, since knowledge is one of the principal characteristics of the Divine.[75] Since the other main characteristics of the Divine are truth and eternity, the attainment of knowledge of the One in the Many would also require strict adherence to truth and an enlargement of the mind from its present narrow and finite foundations. One way, and the way favoured by the Upanishads, is to attain to the intuitive mind which is covered over by the surface mind, *manas*. The Upanishads assert the power of this intuitive mind, *vigyana*, to be immeasurably powerful and capable of taking hold of the surface mind and bending it to its purposes. The intuitive mind comes into operation only in a pure being devoid of desire. Say the Upanishads:

> Those who have known the Vital force of the vital force, the Eye of the eye, the Ear of the ear, and the Mind of the mind, have realized the ancient primordial Brahman. Through the mind alone it is to be realized... (though)... It is unknowable and eternal, the intelligent aspirant after Brahman, knowing about this, attains to intuitive knowledge.[76]

> The mind is spoken of as of two kinds, pure and impure. The impure mind is that which is possessed of desire, and the pure is that which is devoid of desire.[77]

> The desireless one, being free from grief, realizes that glory of Atman through the purity of senses and mind.[78]

> The supreme Divinity can be intuited by a pure and devoted mind.[79]

For the intuitive mind to be able to function, it is necessary for the surface mind to be pacified and made calm. Just as it is not possible to see the bottom of a lake when the surface is disturbed and turbulent, it is not possible for the individual to either realize or effectively operate the intuitive mind till such time as the surface mind is calmed. The intuitive mind, which is the nearest to the sheath of bliss, has the capability to function without using the gross sense organs, since it has access to the subtler and much more powerful controllers of these organs, namely, the inner organs attached to it. It has, therefore the power of direct perception and action and is at the same time not capable of being cognized by the normal surface mind. The practice of truth is the way of the yogis, for truth is austerity, *tapas*.

> The preceptor advises the disciple: speak the truth, walk in the way of the duty, neglect not the study of the Veda.[80]
>
> 'Truth is first (of the various duties)', said the truth speaker, the Rishi, son of Rathitara. 'Tapas is first', said the constant in austerity, the Rishi, son of Purushishta. 'Study and teaching of Veda is first', said Naka, son of Mudgala. That assuredly is *tapas*: indeed, that is *tapas*.[81]

The Upanishads do not only stress truth and austerity as the pre-conditions for yoga but also consider truth as the means of overcoming chaos (*anrita*). In other words truth itself is the yogic way of creating order.[82]

Meditation and Work

The Upanishads further develop the Vedic system by stressing the inner reality of man and thereby taking management from outer only *dharma* to an inward turning of the senses thereby stressing yogic meditative practices and the harmonization of the inner consciousness with the outer action.

Meditation from the earliest times has been practised as a vital part of daily living. In Vedic culture, the day began with the early morning worship of the sun. The sun was but the symbol of the Great Light which man hoped to find within himself. After seeing the visible sun he would close his eyes and search for the inner sun, for the inner light. This is as relevant today as it was thousands of years ago. Today we have forgotten to look inwards for the illumination that is there, and are dismally ignorant, and lost in spiritual darkness. We run hither and thither, but where do we arrive? Consider the ever-increasing hurry and distraction of modern life. Spirituality is not so much denied as merely crowded out.

In fact, the world today is overwhelmed by the voices of blind passion and cruel hatred, of irritability, strife, and misunderstanding. The radical cure of the Upanishads for this outer noise is to find inner silence. And once people learn how to find the inner peace, we shall surely have outward peace and eliminate senseless strife. It will come as a perfect and natural result, and perhaps is the only way in which we shall ever find peace.

Meditation, the art of mental quiet, of yoga, is the fundamental practice in this inner quest. It is essential to whoever seeks to find his spiritual self. The basic principle behind it is simply this: throughout the day we are so busy attending to external things and activities that we never become aware of who it is that is attending to these manifold activities. We just become so immersed in them that we do not even try to know who is being immersed.

Upanishadic meditation has as its primary aim the detachment of this entity or person who is acting, working, walking, moving, from the activities themselves, so that he might get a chance to be truly conscious, to know himself. Hence, the fundamental method advocated by the Upanishads is to direct attention deliberately away from these outward activities and to turn the attention inwards.

Whether in work or at pleasure, we are constantly engaged in external activity. And by external I mean mental activity, which although in appearance internal, is still external, because the working of the intellect is something which the inner being regards as external to itself. Therefore, say the Upanishads, that if you wish to find this innermost being within you, you not only have to turn attention inwards towards the mind, away from the outer action, but you must penetrate still farther inwards away from intellect itself towards that which is behind the intellect. They stress the vital necessity of the practice of meditation as a means of freeing ourselves from the surface life that stresses and enslaves us.

At this point one needs to note that there are many misconceptions about yoga and meditation. People think that the practice of meditation is necessarily going to lead to marvellous supernatural experiences. Well, it may or it may not. They think it is going to develop occult powers.

It may do that, and it may not. They also think that you have to undergo the most ascetic regimes of self-discipline in order to make meditation successful. In fact, the Upanishads make clear that neither extreme asceticism nor a plenitude of riches is the answer. We have to tread the middle way, the path that is "like the razors edge and so difficult to tread."[83]

In the Upanishadic scheme of things, meditative practice leads to work being done with an inner poise and a harmony where right action takes place. According to their thinking, it is in the spiritual nature of human beings to be satisfied and fulfilled. It is work done in the right way that gives us the opportunity to realize this satisfaction by developing the true qualities of our nature. Work properly done is the skillful expression of our total being, our means to create harmony and balance within ourselves and in the world. Through such work we contribute our energy to life, investing our body, our breath, and our mind in creative activity. By exercising our creativity we fulfil our natural role in life, and inspire all beings with the joy of vital participation.

The Upanishads stress the role that work plays in our lives by drawing on every part of our being and bringing our minds, our hearts, and our senses into full play. Yet it is unusual in modern times to become this deeply involved in our work. In today's complex society, we have lost touch with the knowledge of how to use our abilities to lead effective and meaningful lives. In the past, education played an important role in transmitting the knowledge needed to integrate learning and experience, to manifest our inner nature in a practical way. Today, this vital knowledge is no longer passed on. Thus, our general understanding of work is limited, and we seldom realize the deep satisfaction that comes from working skillfully, with our total being.

Perhaps because we do not have to exert our full effort to meet our basic needs, we rarely put our hearts and minds fully into our work; in fact, working just enough to get by has become the norm. Most people do not expect to like their work, much less to do it well, for work is commonly considered as nothing more than a means to an end. Whatever our occupation, we have come to think of work as a time-consuming part of our lives, a duty that cannot be avoided.

If there is a strong enough incentive to work hard, we may do so, but if we look carefully at our motivation, we see it is often narrow in scope, directed primarily toward gaining status, increasing personal power and private domain, protecting the interests of name and family. This kind of self-centered motivation makes it difficult to express and develop our human potential through work. Rather than grounding us in the positive qualities of our nature, the working environment fosters qualities such as competition and manipulation.

The Upanishads assert that life exacts a price for less than full participation. For people lose touch with the human values and qualities that spring naturally from a full engagement in work and life like integrity, honesty, loyalty, responsibility, and cooperation. Without the guidance these qualities give to our lives, we begin to drift, and became prey to an uneasy sense of dissatisfaction. Once we have lost the knowledge of how to ground ourselves in meaningful work, we do not know where to turn to find value in life. The Upanishads take a holistic view and regard work not as a means to an end but as itself being the end. They elucidate a philosophy of work based on greater human understanding, respect for ourselves and others, and an awareness of the qualities and skills that create peace in the world—communication, cooperation and responsibility.

This means being willing to face work openly, to look honestly at our strengths and weaknesses, and to make the changes that will improve our lives. If we genuinely devote our energy to improving our attitude toward work, developing what is truly valuable within us, we can make all of life a joyful experience. The skills we learn while working will set the tone for our growth and give us the means to bring satisfaction and meaning into each moment of our lives, and into the lives of others as well. Working in this way is working with skillful means.

Skillful means in the Upanishadic concept is a three-step process that can be applied to any situation in our lives. The first step is to become aware of the reality of our difficulties, not simply by intellectual acknowledgement, but by honest observation of ourselves. Only in this way we will find the motivation to take the second step—making a firm resolve to change. When we have clearly seen the nature of our problems and have begun to change them, we can share what we have learned with others. This sharing can be the most satisfying experience of all, for there is a deep and lasting joy in seeing others find the means to make their lives fulfilling and productive.

When we use skillful means to realize and strengthen our positive qualities at work, we tap the precious resources that lie awaiting discovery within us. Each of us has the potential to create peace and beauty in the universe. When we develop our abilities and share them with others, we can deeply appreciate their value. This deep appreciation makes life truly worth living, and brings love and joy into all of our actions and experience. By learning to use skillful means in all that we do, we can transform our daily existence into a source of enjoyment and accomplishment that surpasses even our most beautiful dreams.

Conclusion

The Upanishads thus deepen and enlarge on the system of management developed in the Vedas. To the concept of *rita* they add the dimension of *dharma* developed through yogic meditation and a philosophy of work which brings joy and liberates the human being from the stress and strains of life. Management systems based on the Upanishads would stress the need of each person in the organization being in a position to fulfil himself by being able to harmonize himself with the work he has to do. The management structure of such a system would be non-hierarchical and not depend on a centralized command and control system. Since each individual in the system is all the time trying to harmonize his personal goals with the goals of everyone else, the result would be harmony in the system, creativity in action and the optimization of the goals that are placed before the organization.

The Upanishads also lays stress on the principle of stewardship. As we have seen, the Isha Upanishad (1, 2) says: All that is in the cosmos belongs to the Lord. The way to get out of the binding coils of *karma* is to act with detachment and find joy in renouncing the concept of ownership; for all belongs to the Lord.

Peter Block has described stewardship as the:

> Umbrella idea which promises the means of achieving fundamental change in the way we govern our institutions. Stewardship is to hold something in trust for another....
>
> Stewardship is.... the willingness to be accountable for the well-being of the larger organization by operating in service, rather than in control, of those around us. Stated simply, it is accountability without control or compliance.[84]

Block goes on to state that stewardship begins with the willingness to be accountable for same larger body than ourselves—an organization, a community; in engendering partnerships thereby empowering others instead of making them dependent; of trusting others being deeply accountable for the outcomes of an institution, and not acting to define the purpose of others, or controlling them.[85] It is interesting to note the parallelism between Block's ideas and the management system outlined by the Upanishads.

REFERENCES

1. Shwetashwatara Upanishad, 5-6.
2. Rig Veda, 1.24.7.
3. Katha Upanishad, 6.1.
4. Rig Veda, 5.62.1.
5. Aiteraya Upanishad, 4.1.

6. Mahanarayana Upanishad, 1.39, 43, 46, 49, 52, etc.
7. Brihadaranayaka Upanishad, 6.2, 3.
8. Shwetashvatara Upanishad, 4.21, 22.
9. Taittiriya Upanishad, 1.4.
10. Shwetashvatara Upanishad, 3.5.
11. Mundaka Upanishad, 1.2.1.
12. Mundaka Upanishad, 1.2.7.
13. Mundaka Upanishad, 1.2.10 In this connection see also the Chandogya Upanishad, 2.23.1. "Three are the branches of religious duty. Sacrifice, study and gifts are the first, austerity the second, and the life of brahmacharya (self-continence) the third. All these become possessors of meritorious worlds; but he who is firmly established in Brahman attains immortality".
14. "The Self-existent has pierced the door of sense outward, therefore one sees things outwardly and sees not in the inner being. Rarely a sage desiring immortality turns his sight inward and sees the self face to face"—Katha Upanishad, 4.1.
15. Katha Upanishad, 6.12.
16. Taittiriya Upanishad, 2.9.
17. See the third chapter of the Kena Upanishad where neither Agni, nor Vayu, nor Indra can understand or conceive the nature of Brahman.
18. Rig Veda, 10.130.3.
19. Rig Veda, 10.121.8. See also the Yajur Veda, 27.26.

    "Who is the Deity we shall adore with our oblation The Divinity who in His glory surveyed the floods, Giving spiritual power and generating worship. Who is the one God above all gods."
20. Atharva Veda, 11.8.13 and 11.8.32.
21. The Sanskrit word for food is *annam* which means 'that which is eaten or enjoyed'. Philosophically, it means the object which the Spirit or the subject enjoys; in the Upanishads it is often taken to be a synonym for matter.
22. Aiteraya Upanishad, 1.1, 2.
23. Brihadaranayaka Upanishad, 1.4.10.
24. *Ibid.*, 1.4.16.
25. Shwetashvatara Upanishad, 4.9.

26. Amritbindu Upanishad, 18.
27. See Taittiriya Upanishad. Chapter II gives an idea of the involution of Brahman, while Chapter III shows how the evolving soul successively discovers Brahman to be matter, energy, mind, intuitive thought and bliss.
28. Katha Upanishad, 4.1.
29. Mahanarayana Upanishad, 78, 1-12.
30. *Ibid.*, 79. 12, 13.
31. *Bhagavad Gita*, 11.15,16.
32. Mundaka Upanishad, 2.2.5.
33. *Ibid.*, 1.1.7. The concept is akin to the one in the Purusha Sukta of the Rig Veda.
34. "In truth, dear boy, in the beginning there was Being alone, one only, without a second"—Chhandogya Upanishad, 6.2.2.
35. Shwetashvatara Upanishad, 6.6.
36. Taittiriya Upanishad, 2.1-5.
37. Shwetashvatara Upanishad, 6.11.
38. Brihadaranayaka Upanishad, 3.7.15, 1.
39. Shwetashwatara Upanishad, 4.10.
40. Aiteraya Upanishad, 3.1.

    "That indeed is the Atman by which a living being sees form, hears sounds, smells scents, articulates speech, and discriminates what is sweet and what is not. That which is the heart and the mind is the same, as that .... all these are but names of Consciousness."
41. Katha Upanishad, 4.12.10.
42. Mandukya Upanishad, 7.
43. Taittiriya Upanishad, 3.1-6.
44. Shwetashvatara Upanishad, 3.1.
45. *Ibid.*, 4.7, 9.
46. Mundaka Upanishad, 2.1.1.
47. Aiteraya Upanishad, 1.1.
48. Katha Upanishad, 6.4.
49. Prashna Upanishad, 5.3-5.
50. Kaushitaki Upanishad, 3.8.

51. Brihadaranayaka Upanishad, 3.7.15.
52. Katha Upanishad, 2.23. The same verse is also in Mundaka Upanishad, 3.2.3.
53. Shwetashvatara Upanishad, 3.20.
54. Taittiriya Upanishad, 3.6
55. Aiteraya Upanishad, 1.1.
56. Prashna Upanishad, 1.2.
57. Taittiriya Upanishad, 1.9.
58. Brihadaranyaka Upanishad, 5.5.1.
59. Brihadaranayaka Upanishad, 1.4.14.
60. Mundaka Upanishad, 1.2.1.
61. *Ibid.*, 1.1.4,5,6.
62. *Bhagavad Gita*, 6.6, 7.
63. Shvetavastara Upanishad, 3.8.
64. Chhandogya Upanishad, 6.8, 7.
65. Lao Tzu, *Tao Teh Ching*, in *The Tests of Taoism*, James Legge, trans., *Sacred Books of the East*, F. Max Muller, ed., Vol. XXXIX, 1891, reprint edn., New York, Dover Publications, 1962, Ch. 47, p. 89.
66. Taittiriya Upanishad, 2.6.
67. Isha Upanishad, 6.
68. Shwetashvatara Upanishad, 2.13.
69. Mundaka Upanishad, 3.2.2.
70. *Ibid.*, 3.2.5.
71. Chhandogya Upanishad, 6.1.2, 3.
72. Taittiriya Upanishad, 1.11.
73. Shwetashvatara Upanishad, 2.6.
74. Katha Upanishad, 3.12.
75. "Brahman, the Truth, the Knowledge, the Infinite", Taittiriya Upanishad, 2.1.

    "This self is a self of Knowledge",

    Brihadaranayaka Upanishad, 4.3.7.
76. Brihadaranayaka Upanishad, 4.4.18, 19, 21.
77. Amritbindu Upanishad, 1.
78. Katha Upanishad, 2, 20.

79. Shwetashvatara Upanishad, 5.14.
80. Taittiriya Upanishad, 1.11.
81. *Ibid.*, 1.9.
82. Mundaka Upanishad, 3.1.6.

    "Truth conquers, not chaos: By truth is the path laid that leads to the Eternal."
83. Katha Upanishad, 3.14.
84. Peter Block, *Stewardship: Choosing Service over Self-Interest* (San Francisco: Berret-Koehler, 1993) p. xx.
85. *Ibid.*, pp. 6-18.

4

DHARMIC MANAGEMENT: VEDIC SOCIETY

Vedic Management is based, as we have noted, on the following of *dharma*. This leads to the delineation of systems for managing society as well as the State represented in the Veda by the concept of the king. We deal first with the manner in which the Vedic system seeks to manage society. In the next chapter we will deal with the way the State needs to be organized and managed.

In the view of the Vedic seers, socially there was the need for an organism which rested on conscious obedience to higher laws, which made provision for the fact that man is a spiritual being as well as a physical one. According to them, hope for a better world did not lie wholly in a change from within, for that would be too great a demand, nor yet wholly in a change from without, for that also would be too great a demand. It lay rather in a properly proportioned synthesis of the two—the outer and the inner.

If the mass of the people are preoccupied with wresting a livelihood, they can hardly be blamed for being indifferent to a higher spiritual and artistic culture. To them such a culture nust often seem either quite remote or quite imaginary. Apart from their lack of training in the intellect—not to be confused with intelligence—the essential factor in this situation is that they cannot give sufficient attention to such a search. Nor do they have the time to aspire for the truth or its personal realization until they are themselves less hindered by the inevitable dependence on economic conditions. The Veda therefore, does not ignore the economic in elucidating the societal system.

The Vedic sages were not only concerned with the ascetic who consciously and deliberately set out to live with as little as possible. His sef-imposed renunciation, no doubt, has a certain nobility about it, whereas that which is involuntarily borne by the poor usually degrades them. He has taken to an exceptional path for a special purpose and when this is achieved nature may or not eventually bid him return to the middle way as she did with the Buddha. The Vedic seers considered those who can find their happiness only in an environment of poverty as no better than backward-lookers. Higher standerds of living were not considered evil in themselves but needed to be accompanied by spiritual disciplines.

The Vedic seers considered the challenge to man to be one of harmonizing the individual with the societal objectives. While too great a stress on the individual may make a man a crank, a fanatic or an eccentric the opposite of letting social norms dictate to the individual was equally dangerous to the welfare of the individual as it could lead to repression. Social pressures prevent a man from living in conformity with ideas that run counter to them. He must drop his ideas, modify them, or hide them, if he is not to quit the community. Such a compulsory adjustment is neither good for his nerves nor for his character. Strange and unfamiliar ideas which collide with those long held by the society around, or upset those received by convention, come up against human nature, whose first and instinctive answer is to contradict such social and conventional ideas.

It is not pleasant to swim against the current of society in the name of a mystical individualism. The thought of changing routine habits and getting rid of the acquied tendencies of a lifetime appals and irks most people. They have become victims of the habits prevailing in their surroundings and the tendencies themselves have assumed psychological as well as physical existence, having become deep-seated fixations within the subconscious mind. Yet,suffering awaits then if they insist on remaining prisoners of their own worn-out past and will not accommodate themselves to changing conditions and the consequent different outlook required.

Each man is under some degree of tutelage to the mass. Every moment he is acted upon by suggestions from the crowd. He is more or less a slave—slave to social forms, slave to esablished institutions, slave to conventional codes and slave to public opinion. Although this slavery was far worse in former times, even in our own time hardly anyone thinks, feels and acts quite fully and freely out of his individual will alone. He is more likely to think, feel and act largely out of what has been suggested to him by other people. Hence, he hardly ever lives his own independent life or obeys his own inner self but, with everybody, lives the life of the crowd. Even if some part of his attitude towards life is innate, the larger part is not. It is imposed upon him by the instruction and the teaching he has received, by the environment from which he accepts influences, and by the conventional standards to which he conforms. When a world-outlook is so largely fashioned by exernal suggestion, the need of thinking for oneself becomes both a primary virtue and a necessary factor in mental health.

If life becomes exclusively authoritarian, if man submits to having all his thinking, response and living done for him by others, he will eventually become too enervated or debilitated to think, respond and act by his own capacity. For when he is unable to hold a thought unless he has received it from outside, when he does not make a single decision of his own but run to others to make it for him, how can he grow? It is necessary for man to begin to free himself from the societal suggestions imposed upon him, and to start establishing by effort his individual attitude towards life. He has to cast aside passive unthinking acquiescence and become more responsible for his own beliefs and his own life.

The Vedia sages sought to ensure through their concept of society the self-fulfillment of the individuals in that society. This they did through the definition of four orders, four stages and four aims of Vedic society.

The Four Orders

We have seen how the Vedic sages sought to unify society and remove the antipathy between different tribes and races through its concept of the four classes and to integrate society through the concept of *dharma.*

The aim of *dharma* was to understand the outer life of man and subject it to control through inner development. *Dharma* has two sides: The social and the individual; the social deals with the duties assigned to the position of individuals in society as determined by their character and function; the individual deals with the duties relevant to the stage of life, youth, manhood, or old age. The complex matrix which is created by the interaction of individual and social *dharmas* leads to four ideal classes in society. The social *dharma* of the four classes will be dealt with from three different standpoints, the spiritual-social, the ethical-psychological, and the conventional.

The earliest reference to the four classes is in the Purusha Sukta of the Rig Veda, were they are described as having sprung from the body of the Divine Person (the Purusha), from his mouth, arms, thighs, and feet. This poetical image is intended to convey the organic character of society[1]. Man is not only a separated individual but is also in solidarity with his kind. The stress on the universal in its movement towards the goal is the source of man's sociality. Man is also not an abstract entity. He belongs to a certain social group by virtue of his character, behaviour, and function in the community. In the fourfold division of society, the suggestion is that spiritual wisdom, executive power, skilled production, and devoted service are the indispensable elements of any social order. The wise to work out the proper relationships, the powerful to back it by authority, and the skilled to execute it with the help of devoted workers. Dynamism in society (movement) comes from the economic as reperesented by the entrepreneurs (the thighs) and the workers (feet). While the State (arms) regulates and controls, the men of knowledge lay down the basic parameters of the superordinate goals of society.

As the individual is a social being, society is the necessary means by which he attains the full and integral development of his personality. A secure and proper place,in line with his psychological make up, has therefore to be found for him in the community so that he can derive the utmost help from it. Society should not be something alien or an imposition. For then man would either be crushed or rebel against society. The social system should be such as to allow him freedom to develop to his full potential.

By their psycho-ethical natures, human beings fall into four types, those of learning and knowledge, of power and action, the skilled producers, and the labourers. The types are determined by the prominent elements of everyone's nature.

Those who are pre-eminently intellectual are the Brahmins, whose function it is to seek knowledge, communicate it to others, and make it prevail in the world. Their activity is not the pusuit of practial aims in the narrow sense. They should seek joy in the practice of an art like yoga, a science, or a philosophy as a disinterested intellectual pursuit.

While it is the business of the Brahmin to lay down a set of values, draw out a blueprint for social reconstruction, and persuade the world to accept the high ends of life, it is the business of the Kshatriya, the executives, to devise the means for gaining the ends. Also how to regulate, preserve and harmonize the social fabric.

The qualitites that mark the Kshatriya type are a determination from which no danger or difficulty can distract, a dynamic daring character, a nobility of soul which would do nothing sordid or mean, and an unflinching resistance to injustice and oppression. The worshippers of power, the men of brute force, the selfish tyrants are the preversions of this type. The qualities of the Kshatriya are as necessary as those of the Brahmin for the perfection of human nature.

In the above concept, the political or administrative is not conceived as the highest category. The State exists in order that its members may have a good life. It is a social convenience. It is not the judge of its own conduct. As the *Mahabharata* says, though righteousness depends on force, 'it is wrong to say that it is the will of the strong'[2]. The State is not above *dharma*; rather it is bound by *dharma* or the law. It exists essentially for the good of the individual. Kautilya says in the *Arthashastra*, the duty of the State is to ensure to every one the undisturbed enjoyment of what they have acquired *(yogakshema)*[3]. The elevation of the State to a position where it can even justify killing if the ends of state policy so require is totally opposed to the Vedic view. In the *Ramayana* Rama tells Lakshmana: 'I bear arms for the sake of truth. It is not difficult for me to gain this whole universe but I desire not even the suzerainty of the heavens if it is to be through unrighteousness.'[4]

The third class that of Vaishyas, brings into relief the tendency of life to possess and enjoy, to give and take. In its outward action, this power appears as the utilitarian and the practical engaged in commerce and industry. But in fact the *Vaishya* is also required to be marked by humanity and ordered benevolence. The *Vaishya* class being engaged in pursuits where the temptations to the acquisition and hoarding of wealth exist they are expected to develop qualities of humanity and neighbourly service. If they are keen on wealth for its own sake, they are to be 'detested'. It is not their main function to contribute to the spiritual welfare of society or its political power, yet we cannot have these without their cooperation. Practial intelligence and adaptive skill are their chief qualities.

The perversions of this type are familiar to us, as our age is pre-eminently a commercial one. Armament manufacturers, for example, foment discords between nations for the sake of profits. Merchants make millions through the sale of drugs that destroy the body, mind, and soul of people. Commerce and industry, which are the life-blood of the human race, are perverted from their proper use by a false standard of values. Property, according to the Vedic view is a mandate held by its possessors for the common use and benefit of the common weal. The *Bhagavad Gita* (3.12) tells us that we "have a claim only to so much as we would get through *yagya* or sacrifice. If any one desires more, he is a thief."

The fourth variety of human nature finds its outlat in work and service. Labour is the basis of all human activities. While the first three classes are said to be twice born, since they had spiritual growth, the fourth is said to be once born. It only means that the activities of the members of the fourth class are instinctive and not governed by yogic knowledge. Manu (2.46) refers to the yogic knowledge of the three classes when he says.

> The staff of the *Brahmin* shall be made of such length as to reach of the end of his hair; that of a *Kshatriya*, to reach his forehead; (and) that of a *Vaishya*, to reach the (tip of his) nose.

The above is obviously a reference to the seven yogic centres of consciousness *(chakras)* with the *Brahmin* being one who has attained the seventh *(sahasrara)*, the *Kshatriya* the sixth *(agya)*, and the *Vaishya* the fifth *(vishuddha)*. The staff is the 'spiritual spine' in which these *chakras* are supposed to be placed. Frawley has also pointed out the yogic nature of the four classes.[5]

Such a fourfold division of society is not artificial. Our values in life determine how we see the world and how we act within it. We cannot pursue commercial values as the most important thing in life, for example, and yet find the knowledge that liberates our soul. Our commercial preconceptions will colour our knowledge and distort it. They will cause us to use religion for commercial ends. We may pursue wealth as a secondary goal, but if it is our primary goal we cannot expect to understand the truth of things, which requires freedom from the need to gain materially from them.

All cultures have these four groups. Though each culture may not have a specific system for regulating them, they still appear as classes within society. In Western society there are labour, commercial, political, and religious classes;

divisions of society with their own laws and territory, particular need and spokespersons. This is not to say that each group appears in its true form, however. For example, even religion is dominated by political and commercial interests.

It is to be noted that the qualities which are predominant in each of the four classes are not exclusive of one another. As a matter of fact there is no individual who does not possess all these essentials. Classes are marked as wise or heroic, skilled or unskilled, according as one or the other quality predominates in them. None of these can be regarded as complete. The Brahmin cannot serve truth with freedom if he has not moral courae and heroism; if he has not the practical sense to adapt the highest truth to the conditions of actual life and the needs of the different classes of society; or if he has not the sense of service to humanity. Even the man of action, (the Kshatriya) though he is not engaged in the pursuit of wisdom, has to have a sense of direction of society, the aims it has, and the way in which he has to work out the details essential for the realization of those aims. He uses his power for the service of the society. The Vaishya has a general idea of the nature of the social good, has the courage and the enterprise essential for the exploitation of resources, and is anxious to improve the material conditions of life in every conceivable way. The man of labour, (the Shudra) is a part of the social order and strives to serve society through his special function with knowledge, honour, and skill.

According to Radhakrishnan, the fourfold scheme is, in a real sense democratic. Firstly, it insists on the spiritual equality of all men. It assumes that within every human individual there is a self which has the right to grow in its own way, to find itself, and make its life a full and satisfied image and instrument of its being.

Secondly, it makes for individuality in a positive sense.Individuality is attained not through an escape from limitations but through the willing acceptance of obligations.

Thirdly, it points out that all work is socially useful and, from a spiritual standpoint, equally important.

Fourthly, social justice is not a scheme of rights but of opportunities. It is not assumed that all men are alike. Excellence in action as required by the *Bhagavad Gita* (*yogah karmasu kaushalam*, 2.50) is specific to individuals and cannot be universal. Equality in the Vedic sense thus refers to opportunity and not to capacity. While it recognizes that men are unequal in capability, it insists that every human being has the right and the opportunity to contribute to human achivement, as far as his capacity for yogically making the best of life goes.

Fifthly, the essence of democracy is consideration for others. Freedom for the individual means restrictions on absolute power. No one class can make unlimied claims.

Sixthly, the general tendency of men of all classes to strive to climb the social ladder is due to an impression that the position at the top is one of pleasure, profit, and power. But in the Vedic scheme life becomes more difficult as one rises higher. A Brahmin, for example, should do nothing for the sake of power or wealth. A Kshatriya has to even give up his life to maintain *dharma* while the Vaishya is only a trustee of wealth and has to answer to society for all that he does. Only the Shudra is freed from all responsibilities except that of earning his livelihood. The realization that there is increase of social responsibility and diminution of personal enjoyments as one rises in the social ladder, makes a person more satisfied with his place and work in society. Competition in society is thus transformed into cooperation.[6]

The *Bhagavad Gita* goes on to internalize the qualities necessary for each class. Acoording to its psycho-social teaching in the fourfold scheme, each individual has to follow his or her own nature and arrive at possible perfection by a growth from within. The individual is not to be a mere passive instrument of collective life. The individual's action must be determined by his own essential quality (ies). Through the fulfillment of his nature he contributes to his own good of society. Says Sri Krishna;

The works of Brahmins, Kshatriyas, Vaishyas and Shudras are different, in harmony with the qualities born of their nature.

They all attain perfection when they find joy in their work. •

Greater is thy own work, even if this be humble, then the work of another, even if this be great.[7]

The *Bhagavad Gita* (18.42,43,44) also defines the work of the four orders according to their inborn qualities. The classification of work is—for the Brahmin; peace, self-harmony, austerity, purity, forgiveness, righteousness, vision, wisdom and faith; for the Kshatriya; heroic mind, inner fire, constancy, resourcefulness, courage, generosity and noble leadership; for the Vaishya; trade, agriculture and rearing of cattle; and for the Shudra; service.

With the passage of time, the *varna* system degenerted into the caste system as we know it today. As the system degenerated, birth acquired greater importance than the inborn qualities of human beings.

The substitution of the principle of birth for virtue and valour has been the main factor in the process of social crystallization and caste separatism. Birth is said to indicate real, permanent differences in the mental attitudes of men. It is not realized that the fact of ancestry, parentage, and physical birth may not always indicate the nature of the individual. When the obligations of the classes do not spring spontaneously from their inner life, they become mere conventions, departing largely from the maintenance of ethical types.

The truth underlying the system is the conception of right action as a rightly ordered expression of the nature of the individual. Nature assigns to each of us our line and scope in life according to inborn quality and ability to express ourselves. Nowhere is it suggested that one should follow one's hereditary occupation without regard to one's personal bent and capacities. The caste system is a degeneration of the ethical class (*varna*) idea. Though idealistic in its origin, beneficient in large tracts of its history, still helpful in some ways, it has grown out of harmony with our present conditions, owing to arrested development and lack of elasticity.

The Four Stages and Four Aims of Life

The Vedic scheme does not leave the growth of the individual entirely to his unaided initiative but gives him a framework for guidance. Human life is represented as consisting of four consecutive stages, of which the first three fall within the jurisdiction of society. These stages apply to everyone in the social structure.

The four stages are those of the student, the householder, the social worker (called forest dweller in ancient times) and the *sannyasi* or one who leaves the material world in search of self-realization.

Human offspring are the most helpless of all living creatures. In the absence of parental care, their chances of survival are little. The tending has to be continued for a long period, till the child reaches manhood. Also the higher the cultural level of society the longer is the period required for education. This is the time that man is required to spend as a student.

The aim of Vedic education was not to impose a stereotyped rule of conduct but to help the child to develop his nature, to change him from within rather than crush him from without. The knowledge imparted had not only to fit man for his role in life but give him a general idea of the conditions of spiritual life.

The householder contributes to society by marrying, raising a family and earning his livelihood by following the profession most suited to his temperament. Man attains his full being only by living in harmonious social relationships. Sex is a normal human function concerned with the perpetuation of the race. Marriage, love and motherhood are glorified in the Veda. The wife has an equal position with the husband in all domestic and religious concerns. Every woman has a right to marry and have a home. The things of spirit are in part dependent on the satisfaction of the body. The physical and the economic being, though not important in themselves, are important as means to the life of spirit. The position of householder is glorified by Manu who regards the householder as the mainstay of all the other classes.

> As all living creatures subsist by receiving support from the air, even so (the members of) all orders subsist by receiving support from the householder.
>
> Because men of the three (other) orders are daily supported by the householder with (gifts of) sacred knowledge and food, therefore (the order of) householders is the most excellent order (3,77,78).[8]

The object of man is not merely to be born, to grow up, marry, earn a livelihood, found a family, support it and pass away. That would be a physical life almost akin to the life of an animal. The object has to be to grow vertically into a mental and spiritual life transcending the animal instincts. This has to be through social service. When the children get settled and no more want his attention, a man should retire with his wife from active life to serve society. This both purifies and enables him to repay his debt to society.

A *sannyasn* renounces all possessions, distinctions of caste, and practices of religion. As he has already purified himself through social service, he is able to give his soul the largest scope and throw all his powers into the free movement of his spirit. He does not merely formulate the conception of high living but lives it, adhering to the famous rule; 'The world is my country; to do good my religion'.Regarding all with an equal eye he is friendly to all living beings and does not injure any living creature, human or animal, either by act, word, or thought. He also renounces all attachments. A freedom and fearlessness of spirit, an immensity of courage, a love that lavishes itself without demand of return are the perfections he seeks.

Having defined the four orders and the four stages that every one has to follow, the Vedci sages turned their attention as to how to harmonize the normal instincts of man with the highest spiritual end. This they did by laying down the main values to be followed in life as; pleasure *(kama)*, wealth *(artha)*, virtue *(dharma)*, and liberation *(moksha)*. These values create four mental natures. If we pursue pleasure only we develop a servile mentality, as we become dependent upon external sources of enjoyment and stimulation. If we pursue wealth alone we develop a commercial mentality and judge the world in terms of property and prices. If we pursue fame or power we develop a political or militaristic mentaliy and its distinctions of ranks and status. So these need to be moderated and regulated by an ethical attitude, by *dharma*. The pursuit of liberation and *moksha*, helps to develop a spiritual mentality and to seek the higher knowledge.

The four objectives, namely, virtue, wealth, pleasure, and liberation fall into outer activity and inner poise. Wealth and pleasure belong to the way of activity; liberation to the internal way of renunciation; virtue *(dharma)* is common to both. Of these four, liberation is the ultimate value; the rest are instrumental, being preparatory to the knowledge of truth, which alone makes man free.

In grading the various objectives, however, Kautilya in the *Arthashastra* (1.7.6-7) gives top priority to *artha* since all others are dependent on it. But while accepting the spontaneous activites of earning wealth and desire the Vedic system asserts that their full value cannot be realized without a rule, a guidance, a restraint. *Dharma* is considered by them as the sine qua non for the supreme good, as no spiritual unfoldment is possible without if. Not only that; it is indispensable to material welfare also. Any progress in life, material as well as spiritual, must be based on man's moral worth. So virtue *(dharma)* and not wealth, is considered to be the primary object of life. According to Manu, the Veda is the primary source of *dharma*.[9]

Dharma, or the art of ethical living, is what gives coherence and direction ot the different activities of life. It is the complete rule of life, the harmony of the whole man who finds a right and just law of his living. Each man and group, each activity of soul, mind, life, and body, has its *dharma*. Thus, while man is justified in satisfying his desires, to wholly conform to the dictates is not, and cannot be, the law of his being. He can only get the best out of them if he conforms to the *dharma* which tells us that, while our life is in the first instance for our own satisfaction, it is more essentially for the good of the community. The community of man is the whole world and so the *Bhagavad Gita* (3.25) advises that "the wise man should work unattached for loksangraha, or the welfare of all, and world-solidarity."

The aim relating to weath and material well-being *(artha)* while not its own end helps to sustain and enrich life. There was never in India a national idea of poverty or squalor. Spiritual life finds full scope only in communities with a certain degree of freedom from sordidness. Lives that are strained and starved cannot be religious except in a rudimentary way. Economic insecurity and individual freedom do not go together.

There is a widely prevalent idea that the Vedic view concedes no reality to life, that it despises vital aims and sarisfactions, that it gives no inspiring motive to human effort. There is little in Vedic thought to support the view that one has to attain spiritual freedom by means of abstaining from normal life. On the other hand, it lays down that we must pass throught the normal life conscientiously and with knowledge, work out its values,and accept its enjoyments (*kama*). Spiritual life is an integration of man's being in its depth and breadth, in its capacity for deep meditation as well as enjoyment of physical life. *Kama* refers to the emotional being of man, his feelings and desires. If man is denied his emotional life, he becomes a prey to repressive introspection as has been pointed out by Freud. Sri Krishna says to Arjuna, "I am *kama* which is not divorced from *dharma*".[10] It is not desire that is to be rooted out but its unrestrained activity.

Also, in life the outer goals commonly mask themselves as the inner. This is the great tragedy from which the greatest confusion arises. We veil our seeking of wealth and power as a pursuit of truth or as serving religion.Religion is used as a mask for promoting commercial and political goals. This is not something done consciously. Most of the time we are victims of our own desires, which we blindly transfer into the religious realm where they have no place.

It is to prevent such intermingling of the sacred and profane from taking place that the sages have created the concept of the Brahmin who, according to Manu, "is forbidden from taking service under a king," "has to acquire knowledge, teach and give alms",[12] and "seek a means of bare subsistence which causes no pain to others".[13] Those who lay down the law, therefore, are to have no link with the State and are to live in poverty. This enables them to be objective in their dealings with the powerful and the wealthy.

The four ends of life point to the different sides of human nature, the intellectual and the ethical, the economic, the instinctive and the emotional, and the spiritual. There is implanted in man's fundamental being a spiritual capacity. He becomes completely human only when his sensibility to spirit is awakened. So long as man's life iis limited to science, technical invention, and socioeconomic programmes, he is incomplete. If we are unfair and unkind to one another, unhappy in personal relationships,and lacking in mutual understanding, life cannot be complete. We have to get out of remaining too much on the surface of life and regain contact with its depths.

Such a view may not readily appeal to modern man. To him economic values rather than the moral values are of prime importance. He thinks that money can solve the problems of life more effectively than morality. And for gaining wealth also, he finds cleverness and technincal devices more effective than honesty. In his view, moral scruples considerably hamper worldly sucess. He believes he has a greater chance for securing prosperity and happiness by sacrificing moral principles than by adhering to them. The ancient seers, however, saw things differently.Manu (2.224) says:

> Some declare that the chief good consists in the acquisition of spiritual merit and wealth, others place it in the gratification of desire and the acquisition of wealth, others in the acquisition of spiritual merit alone,

while some say that the acquisition of wealth alone is the chief good here; but the correct decision is that it consists of the aggregate of all three.

It is not that the sages looked down on the acquisition of wealth and pleasures but wanted these to be integrated and harmonized with spiritual pursuits. It is in this connection that *dharma*, especially *swadharma*, becomes necessary.

The Vedic sages expect a person to try and prosper in this world by the honest and efficient discharge of the duties of his station in life. Wealth or position gained by any other means is considered insecure and may even be harmful. Worldly success without corresponding inner development in the Vedic system is not regarded as a mark of progress; for the secret of strength, wisdom, freedom, and happiness is not in one's external resources but in one's inner paise and serenity. Wealth does not bring wisdom. Mastery over physical nature does not lead to self-mastery, nor does sense enjoyment assure health and happiness.

It must not be forgotten that humanity's problems are mainly psychological rather than biological. Generally speaking, the wealthy have more agonies than those who live in hardship and privation. As long as a person has moral weakness, such as jealousy, hatred, anger fear, pride lust, or greed, one will have trouble wherever one may be.A fortune-seeker may amass huge wealth, yet without inner light it is not possible to find the right way through life. An aggressor may conquer territory after territory and rule over the destinies of millions of human beings, yet he remains a slave to his passions and impulses. A queen may indulge in all the comforts and luxuries of the world, yet a streak of jealousy or vanity can make her miserable for life. The answer in Vedic thought is, therefore, not to be unidimensional in one's attitude but to integrate the physical, the material and spiritual in a harmonious manner.

This was meant to be achieved through the organization of Vedic society as a complex and subtle arrangement of human life through its concept of the four orders of communal life, the four stages of individual life, and the four aims that everyone had to follow.

Human life was also conceived in the Veda to be a process of gradual growth. So provisions were made in such a way that each stage of growth was first stabilized before leading gradually to the next higher stage. Thus, in the four major stages recognized, each state was presented with a set of ideals to be pursued and fulfilled. Each stage had its own *dharma*. These four, namely, *brahmacharya* (student life), *grihastha* (balance of enjoyment and performance of duties appropriate to the householder), the *vanaprashta* (the preparation to leave ordinary life by enlargement, by travel, and by detachment), and *sannyasa* (final renunciation of ordinary life for the exclusive pursuit of spiritual life), were conceived as psychological stages of a large and flexible framework for the growth of the individual. And the general conditions of social life were so organized as to provide to each individual the necessary help needed at a given stage of growth.

This was further facilitated by the recognition of four (ideal) types of temperaments among people with corresponding social functions, resulting in four divisions of the people in a composite social life. These four, the Brahmin (with the temperament that seeks knowledge and fulfills itself in the function of the seeker of knowledge and the teacher), the Kshatriya (with the temperament of power, courage, action and heroism which fulfills itself in the function of the ruler and the administrator), the Vaishya (with the temperament of mutuality, harmony and inter-change that fulfills itself in the function of commerce and inter relationships), and Shudra (with the temperament of technical skill, service and physical labour), were the recognized types, each one requiring a stable field of education, experience and expression. Each type had its own *dharma*, and each had the suitable means of growth not only within its own limits, but also so as to rise higher to the next ascending type of temperament and function.

The Vedic view of the individusl and his relation to

society in its ideal form can be best brought out by a refrence to the synthesis and gradation of:

- the fourfold object of life with its stress on virtuous and ethical living *(dharma)*, earning of wealth *(artha)*, happiness and pleasure *(kama)*, and liberation *(moksha)*;
- the fourfold order of society, consisting of the man of learning (Brahmin), of executive power (Kshatriya), of skilled productivity (Vaishya), and of service (Shudra); and
- the fourfold succession of the stages of life, namely, student *(brahmachari)*, householder *(grihastha)*, social servant *(vanaprashta)*, and the suprasocial *(sannyasin)*.

The Vedic social structure was thus conceived on three interlinked axes with four dimensions each, namely, the objectives of life, the ideal order of society, and the stages of life. The last is in the time dimension, while the first two are in social space. In this three dimensional concept, equality (which is an important aspect of unity) is sought, as we shall presently see, not in the means but in the end, that is, liberation or *moksha*. This liberation is attainable to everyone not on the basis of psycho-technical capacity or position in the social order (which are bound to be different and so unequal), but in how well each individual utilizes his abilities and opportunities. As Sri Krishna says to Arjuna:

> He who makes pure his work by yoga, who watches over his soul, who by wisdom destroys his doubts, is the liberated man.[14]

The three axes can also be looked at in a systems analytical framework. The fourfold order of society *(varna)* and the four stages of life *(ashrama)* form a 4x4 matrix which characterizes the social structure. And in fact the two have always been referred to together as *Varnashrama*. [15] Every element of the social matrix has a quadruple objective function laid down by the ends to be attained *(purushartha)*. It will thus be seen that everyone in the social system has to have knowledge (so that he can understand *dharma*), means of livelihood *(artha)*, enjoyment *(kama)* so that he can ultimately liberate himself from all social bonds *(moksha)*. In other words, every individual has to have the possibility of living a full life. Besides the multiple objective function means that no generalized and unique answer is possible for everyone; it varies from individual to individual. This leads to a decentralized system where harmony is attained through everyone following the same superordinate goals, that is, the ethical means of *dharma* so as to ultimately get liberated.

It is instructive to study human values in the light of the comprehensive concept of the four objectives. These are as we have noted, *dharma, artha, kama* and *moksha*. In its scale of values, the Vedic system finds an honoured place for all desires and urges of man, from the material and sensory to the moral, ethical, and super-sensory or transcendental. The Sanskrit word and concept, *kama*, desire, constitutes the entire range of human cravings and satisfactions at the sensory level; it is the first of the aims of human life. The second aim is *artha*, wealth, which is the instrument for the satisfaction of *kama*. The third aim is *dharma*, which means ethical sense, and which helps to discipline and regulate the pursuit of the first and the second aims, so that all persons in a society get the opportunity to satisfy their urge for them. Human values in socio-economic management proceed from this third aim of *dharma;* though third in order from the point of view of human experience, it is put first in all enmerations, due to its primacy and importance. This *dharma* is essentially what manifests spontaneously as a by-product of man's inner growth, of man's spiritual growth, from the freedom of individuality to the freedom and social responsibility of personality. The integrated following of the three aims leads to liberation, *moksha*.

The scheme of the objectives of life, classes, and stages has for its aim the development of the individual. It helps him to order and organize his life instead of leaving it as a bundle of incompatible desires. It looks upon him, not as a mere individual, but as a member of a social group which reflects in its organization the scheme of values for the realization of which the group exists. By spiritual education and social discipline the individual is helped to develop the inner conviction essential for social stability. But throughout there is insistence on the fact that the highest values are suprasocial and truly universal.

The societal structure, it may be noted, is modelled on the triune aspect of the One, the *Sacchidananda* (Existence-Consciousness-Beatitude). The three ends man seeks are a full life, knowledge and happiness, and these are the earthly counterparts of *Sacchidananda*. This gives to man three rights: the right to life, the right to knowledge and the right to happiness. The first right has to be provided by the state or society, the second by education and the third by the economic system.

The Vedic Socio-economic System

Of the four objectives of the Vedic societal system, the earning of wealth *(artha)* is juxtaposed between ethics and virtue *(dharma)* and the pursuit of happiness *(kama)*. This has been referred to in the literature as the threefold path *(trivarga)* and, according to Manu, it is the integrated and harmonized pursuit of all three that leads to the supreme good.[16] In the Vedic view, therefore, economics cannot be divorced from ethics and the pursuit of happiness: Man's objectives have to be conceived in a large intersecting set involving ethics, economics and happiness.

Happiness is essentially an emotional or spiritual experience of the individual, though influenced by external circumstances. It is a subjective state and an empirical fact. Ethics, on the other hand, is normative and deals with conduct. Ethical norms prescribe the right conduct for individuals so that one can relate well to one's fellow beings individually and collectively. Ethics is also the organization of conduct in terms of notions like good, right or welfare. In this sense, ethics is concerned with, not merely actual conduct, but conduct as it should be, that is, ideals. Economic values involve the understanding of econmic phenomena in addition to the way human beings organize their material, as opposed to spiritual life.

To the Vedic sages, happiness and peace were closely interlinked. One was not attainable without the other. The chant that every Hindu has to make every day is;

> May all be happy and healthy; may all progress spiritually; may nobody be prey to unhappiness. Let there be peace in the universe.[17]

The Sanskrit word *sukkha* (translated happy in the above verse) has many meanings, for example, it may mean pleasure, happiness, well-being, welfare, and a lot more. This word is the opposite of *dukkha* (translated unhappiness in the verse) which means sadness, deprivtion, unhappiness and a lot more. The English words given as meanings for *sukkha* and *dukkha* are not all synonymous: for example, one can be 'happy' in a state of inebriation, but that may not be tantamount to his real well-being. However, the ultimate aim of socio-economic activities has something to do with *sukkha*, that is to say, as a result of all the labour, people should feel happy or fulfilled, or get a sense of well-being, or an amalgam of all three.

The idea that pleasure or happiness is the highest good that human beings should strive for was widely prevalent in the ancient and medieval worlds. All the Greek thinkers, for example, had subscribed to one or other variants of this view. But the Vedic sages went beyond happiness narrowly defined. They felt that beatitude should be the ultimate goal of human beings. They thought in terms of integration of pleasure *(sukkha)*, happiness *(priti)* and bliss *(ananda)*. Pleasure was a desirable sentiment, as against other disagreeable experiences such as pain, deprivation, and so on, while happiness and bliss were the next higher stages to be achieved. Of the four objectives posited by the sages, namely, *dharma*, *artha*, *kama*, and *moksha*, the latter three involve the above mentioned happiness, pleasure and bliss.

It is of course easy to understand why individuals everywhere in the past and present have preferred happiness, and think of it as the ideal to aspire for. It is, simply stated, an obviously preferred mental state. Because even a masochist is 'enjoying' while undergoing pain, since to him *that* is happiness! The real problem is to understand the nature of happiness. What kind of happiness or pleasure should be tried for. It is when these have to be defined that problems arise.

The Vedic sages seem to have made a distinction between happiness in relation to the soul and to the body. In other words, happiness secured through material goods and services, and happiness as a result of non-material spiritual endeavours. The Hindu sages distinguished between the good *(shreyas)* and the pleasant *(preyas)*. As the Katha Upanishad says:

> One thing is the good *(shreyas)* and quite another thing is the pleasant *(preyas)*, and both seize upon a man with different meanings. Of these, whosever takes the good, it is well with him; whereas he falls from the aim of life who chooses the pleasant.
>
> The good and the pleasant come to a man and the thoughtful mind turns all around them and distinguishes. The wise chooses out the good from the pleasant, but the dull soul chooses the pleasant rather then the getting of his good and its having.[18]

On a surface view of the matter it would appear that both the good and the pleasant cannot be pursued at the same time. There is hardly any doubt that, since the Vedic times, people have hankered after material things. There are many passages in the Vedic texts seeking material things such as grain, cows, horses chariots, gold and so on. But we must also remember that Vedic hymns are not only poetry but mystic poetry that was perfected over a long process of meditation.

It is important to understand, therefore, that while the spiritual quest may have been the goal of the sages who composed the hymns, the same was not the case for others who had to live in the world. This was something well understood by the seers of the Vedas. They felt that man could live a good and happy life, and did not need to escape from the world. What they emphasized was the wholeness of being, from communion bringing about right living as implied in the Vedic prayer:

"Grant us riches that cause prosperity for all".[19]

Similar was the thinking of the Upanishads which came after the Vedas. The Upanishads postulated that happiness based solely on material goods was not possible. The story of Nachiketas in the *Katha Upanishad* makes this clear:

> Yama (God of Death) to Nachiketas: Choose sons and grandsons, choose much cattle and elephants and gold and horses; choose a mighty reach of earth and thyself live for as many years as thou listest.
>
> Yea, all desires that are hard to win in the world of mortals, all available at thy pleasure; lo these delectable woman with their chariots and their bugles, whose like are not to be won by men, these I will give thee...
>
> Nachiketas's reply is significant:
>
> These things last till tomorrow, O Death, for they wear out the vigour of all the senses. Even the whole of life is short. Keep the horses, keep dance and song for thyself.
>
> No man can be made happy by wealth alone, we already possess wealth, having seen thee.[20]

This raises the question as to how a human being is to enjoy the material pleasures of life. The Isha Upanishad has this to say:

> In the heart of the all things, of whatever there is in the universe, dwells the Lord. He alone is the reality. Wherefore renouncing vain appearances, rejoice in him. Covet no man's wealth.[21]

Enjoyment through renunciation of desires and the regarding of all material wealth as belonging to the Lord is the suggested answer. Also to see one's actions as part of an integrated whole encompassing both the material and the spiritual ends, and against the backdrop of infinity, of the One who is everywhere. It means going beyond me and thee, mine and thine.

Commenting on the above verse, Shri Aurobindo has this to say,

> so long as the difference between I and you exists, hatred cannot cease, covetousness cannot cease, war cannot cease, evil and sin cannot cease, and because sin cannot cease, sorrow and misery cannot cease. This is the eternal maya that makes a mock of all materialistic schemes for a materialistic paradise upon earth. Paradise cannot be made upon the basis of food and drink, upon the equal division of goods or even upon the common possession of goods, for always the mine and thine, the greed, the hate, will return again if not between this man and that man, yet between this community and that community.

The answer, according to Sri Aurobindo, is to see oneself as part of the whole of creation:

> To see your Self in all creatures and all creatures in your Self—that is the unshakable foundation of all religion. love, patriotism, philanthrophy, humanity, of everything which rises above selfishness and gross utility.[22]

Selfishness is nothing but mistaking the body for the Self and seeking its gratification and thus seeking a gross narrow and transient pleasure, instead of the stainless bliss of one's true Self. By emphasizing the 'Self' as well as de-emphasizing the material basis of the individual, Vedic philosophy harmoniously linked the individual with society. Thus, classical Hindu ethics avoided "the two extremes, viz. considering society to be all-important and over-emphasizing the importance of the individual by overlooking the effect that society has on individual development".[23]

One finds in the earliest Indian writings references to correct behaviour. Among the ideals of living giving to others was the ideal to be aimed at. Nowhere do we find accumulation of property castigated as a vice, but it was considered wrong not to share one's riches with others. The Rig Veda is clear on the need for being generous:

> The gods surely did not ordain hunger alone for slaughter; various deaths reach the man who is well-fed. The riches of the man who gives fully do not run out, but the miser finds no one with sympathy.

The man with food who hardens his heart against the poor man who comes to him suffering and searching for nourishment—though in the past he had made use of him—he surely finds no one with sympathy.

The man who is truly generous gives to the beggar who approaches him thin and in search of food. He puts himelf at the service of the man who calls to him from the road, and makes him a friend for times to come. That man is no friend who does not give of his own nourishment to his friend, the companion at his side. Let the friend turn away from him; this is not his dwelling place. Let him find another man who gives freely, even if he be a stranger.

...Riches roll like the wheels of a chariot, turning from one to the other.

...The man who eats alone brings troubles on himself alone.[24]

The Brihadaranyaka Upanishad develops on the above. It says that for human beings there are three important duties: to be self controlled, to be charitable and to be compassionate. Self control conquers heaven, charity the earth and compassion the lower worlds. These are also in the language of the Upanishad referred to as the worlds of the *devas* (the spiritual forces), men and *asuras* (the forces of materialism).[25]

The Upanishads considered the earning of wealth very much as an integral part of ethics.Virtue *(dharma)* means inner excellence and worthiness for the performance of an individual's duties towards himself and others. So it includes intellectual abilities as well. The *smritis* or *dharmashastras*,[26] which laid down detailed rules on the conduct of individuals, elaborated on this concept. Manu, for example, enumerates wisdom and knowledge under virtue (*dharma*), which according to him, consists of ten qualities, namely, contentment, forgiveness, uprightness, non-stealing, cleanliness, self-control, wisdom, knowledge, truth, and equanimity.[27] The reference to non-stealing is interesting; it puts a constraint on unfair economic dealings with others for the purpose of accumulation of wealth by insisting that they be equitable and 'right'.

As we have seen, the Vedic thinkers wanted the early part of life to be devoted exclusively to the cultivation of virtue while being a student (*brahmachari*). In this period moral development was emphasized more than the intellectual; unlike the modern system of education which stresses intellectual growth, ignoring the moral. In the Taittiriya Upanishad we find a teacher giving the following instruction to his pupil after teaching him all the Veda:

> Speak the truth. Do your duties. Swerve not from your study. After giving the teacher the gift liked by him,[28] you shall marry and have children. Never deviate from truth. Never fail in your duty. Never neglect your welfare. Never neglect your *prosperity*. Never neglect study and teaching. Do not disregard your duties toward God and the ancestors. Serve the mother as a god. Serve the father as a god. Serve the teacher as a god. Serve the guest as a god. You should do such deeds as are unreproachable, and not others. You should do such virtuous deeds as we have done, and not others (emphasis added).[29]

The stress on not neglecting prosperity is to be noted. In this one verse, all the obligations of a human being—to God, his ancestors, mother, father, teachers and the rest of humanity—are elucidated. This is what *dharma* in all its complexity is: the discharge of one's obligation to others through the proper and disinterested discharge of one's duty.

Implicit in the above is the need to respect the *trivarga*:[30] *dharma*, *artha* and *kama*—of others. In this connection, *artha* is understood to stand for material well-being as well as the means of securing such well-being, particularly wealth. Like the other two goals of *trivarga*, *artha* also has primarily the individual in view. It is the individual who is to pursue *artha* as one of the goals of his life. Now, an essential condition of a man's material well-being is security of livelihood. This is probably the reason why *artha* is defined as *vritti* or livelihood by Kautilya in the *Arthashastra*. *Kautilya* also declares *artha* as the most important of the three since the other two are dependent on it.[31]

Vedic Society and Management

The Vedic thought created a societal system in which the prime consideration was to be the self-fulfillment of the individual by which he was to be enabled to attain the highest happiness possible. This was to be achieved by the following of *dharma* by everyone, a *dharma* in which the consciousness of the individual was to be enlarged to embrace his neightbours, his class, his nation and ultimately the whole world. In this way, society would be stable and peaceful, while the individual attained the highest possible state of happiness.

There is no doubt that the Vedic social order is a normative and idealistic schemata. It is also suffused with value. For the original concept of the *chaturvarna* (four orders) was in the Vedas symbolic and spiritual. In the Vedic idea, the four orders represented the Divine in four aspects, the Divine as knowledge, the Divine as power, the Divine as production, enjoyment and mutuality, and the Divine as service, obedience and work.

In later times, however, rigidities and prohibitions entered and the whole system ultimately declined into rigid classifications into codes of privileges and prohibitions. The *ashrama* system (the system of stages of life) had broken down much earlier, but the *varna* system (the system of classification in society) confinued a little longer, but it began to crystallize itself and gradually degraded itself into a rigid caste system.

The caste system is still persistent. Many regard this system to be pernicious and injurious to the individual and to the society, and needs to be got rid of.

According to Joshi, modern times are fast and there is

in every field an accelerated speed of development. This requires a new social organization. The survival or revival of the past is neither desirable nor practicable. The system of classification of society into the fourfold order is neither the principle of the ideal age of the perfected truth nor of the iron age (called in Indian terminology *kaliyuga*). In other words, the *varna* system is appropriate only to the intermediate ages like the *treta* and the *dwapara*. In the former, the social order is maintained by will power and force of character, and in the latter, by law, arrangement and fixed convention. In the present age, with a constant pressure for the accelerated and integrated growth of man, the demand can be fulfilled only by an attempt at a new order in which each individual is given opportunities and facilities to develop on his line of development towards his integral fullness.[32]

It seems to me that we need to distinguish between the system as develop by Vedic thought in a normative fashion and the present degenerate caste system. Throughout history the eternal verities of the normative system have been put into the context of the present through the *smritis* and the *dharmashastras*. Perhaps there is need for a *dharmashastra* to meet the needs of today. This may be the answer and not the abolition of system of the Vedic social order as originally conceived.

REFERENCES

1. Rig Veda, 1.90.11, 12. See also *laws of Manu*, (1.31), tr. by G. Buhler, 1886, reprinted 1982 (Delhi: Motilal Banarasidas) p. 13, which states: "But for the sake of the prosperity of the worlds, He caused the *brahmin*, the *kshatriya*, the *vaishya* and the *shudra* to proceed from His mouth, His arms, His thighs and His feet." In later citation *Laws of Manu* will be referred to as Manu.
2. *Mahabharata*, 3.134.3.
3. R.P. Kangle, *Kautilya's Arthashastra*, (Delhi: Motilal Banarasidas, 1992), p. 116.
4. *Valmiki's Ramayana*, 2.97. 6-7.

5. David Frawley, *Gods, Sages and Kings* (Delhi: Motilal Banarsidas, 1995) pp. 261-62.
6. S. Radhakrishna, *Eastern Religions and Western Thought* (London: Oxford University Press, 1939 reprint 1991), pp. 267-68.
7. *Bhagavad Gita*, 18.41, 45, 47.
8. Manu, p. 89.
9. Manu, 2.6.
10. *Bhagavad Gita*, 7.11.
11. Manu, 3.64, 153.
12. *Ibid.*, 1.82.
13. *Ibid.*, 4.2.3.
14. *Bhagavad Gita*, 4.41.
15. R.P. Kangle, *Kautilya's Arthashatra*, note, 3, 13.4.62.
16. Manu, 2.224.
17. The Sanskrit chant is,

    sarve bhavantu sukkhinah

    sarve santu niramayah

    sarve bhadrani pashyantu

    ma kashchid dukkha bagh bhavet

    om shanti, shanti, shanti
18. Katha Upanishad, 2.1.2. The translation is by Sri Aurobindo, *The Upanishads: Texts, Translations and Commentaries*, (Pondicherry: Aurobindo Ashram, 1986) p. 220.
19. Rig Veda, 1.79.9.
20. Katha Upanishad, 1.23, 25, 26, 27. Translation by Sri Aurobindo, note 18.
21. Isha Upanishad, verse 1.
22. Sri Aurobindo, note 18.
23. S. Gopalan, *Hindu Social Philosophy* (Delhi: Wiley Eastern 1979) p. 55.
24. Rig Veda, 10.117. 1-6.
25. See Brihadarnayaka Upanishad, 5.2.1-3.
26. The word *smiriti* means to remember or recall. The idea

was to recall the moral codes (*dharmashastras*) before taking any action.

27. Manu, 6.92.
28. In Vedic times the students lived with the teacher and received education free of all charges. They only paid him when they left with something inexpensive.
29. Taittiriya Upanishad, 1.11.1, 2.
30. *Trivarga* means the threefold way.
31. Kangle, note 3, Vol. III, p. 1.
32. Joshi, Kireet, *The Veda and Indian Culture* (Delhi: Motilal Banarasidas, 1992) pp. 54-55.

5

DHARMIC MANAGEMENT: THE ART OF GOVERNANCE

The Vedas and the Upanishads elucidated a normative or ideal system of management of society. Such a system was highly decentralized and depended on every person following his *dharma* towards the attainment of the three *purusharthas*, or aims of life, and which could ultimately result in liberation or *moksha*, the fourth and final *purushartha*. Coordination and integration of the system was to be attained by each individual trying to attain harmony with everybody else in the system.

In such a situation no regulatory authority or State was obviously necessary. But as pointed out in the Shantiparvan chapter of the *Mahabharata*, while at the beginning of creation, in the Golden Age, men acted according to *dharma* though there was no ruler nor any punishment, the position changed in course of time as men were overcome by delusion, greed, love of pleasures and other base passions, and that in consequence there was anarchy everywhere. The gods were filled with apprehension and approached Brahma, the Creator, to seek a way out. The latter reassured them and composed a treatise in order that an orderly and peaceful existence may be ensured for men on earth. The treatise, it is said, in addition to the *trivarga* of *dharma*, *artha* and *kama* dealt with state policy and the theory of punishment so that men did not deviate from the right path.[1] Thus, did the *dharmashastras* lay down the art of governance for Vedic society.

The *dharmashtras* or *smritis*, of which the *Manusmriti* or the Laws of Manu and Kautilya's *Arthashastra* are prime examples, have been considered here in addition to the *Mahabharata* and the *Ramayana*, to see how the mode of governance necessary for the Vedic society is delineated.

All the three treatises take the cosmos and not man as the starting point for delineating *dharma*. According to them, the cosmos consists of different orders of being ranging from the material through the animal to the human, each autonomous and standing in a complex pattern of relationships with the rest within a larger framework. The cosmos is thus polycentric and without a dominant centre to which the rest of the universe could be instrumentally related. Since man represented only one order of being, obviously he could not be the centre of the universe. And since they conceived the cosmic Spirit as a principle of order and not as a Creator, it too lacked the separateness, transcendence and independence necessary to constitute one. Man was an integral part of the cosmos, tied to it by a million bonds and incomprehensible outside of it. Since he was internally and necessarily related to the rest of its members, he was seen not as a bearer of properties but as being in a world of relationships, a holistic being, and a member of such increasingly wider wholes as the family, the clan, the community, mankind, the material world and the all-encopassing cosmos. Each whole was self-contained but not self-sufficient, and was both autonomous and a significator of the larger whole of which it was a part.

The *dharmashastras* maintain that since the cosmic Spirit informs and structures the universe, all creation is divine and one. It was one in both the substantial and systemic senses, the former because it shared a common spiritual essence, the latter because it constituted an organically interdependent system and formed a coherent whole. The universe was thus a 'partnership' between its constituent parts and their common heritage. Since man's very survival required it, he might take from the universe what he needed to live in moderate comfort but no more and only under certain conditions. He had no right to violate the integrity of the other orders of being and disturb their balance and rhythm. Since nature constantly reproduced and replenished itself, he might draw on its resources but had no right to undermine its regenerative capacity.

The *smritis*, in line with the teachings of the *Bhagavad Gita*[2], regarded the universe as one vast *yagya*, a system of uncoerced and interrelated offerings. Also since mankind constituted an organic whole and men were necessarily interdependent, every human action was both self- and other-regarding. Directly or indirectly, visibly or invisibly, it affected the collective ethos and shaped the quality of the prevailing pattern of human relationships. We cannot see this, nearsighted as we are, but it remains an inescapable feature of the necessarily interdependent world. The way to integrate all constituents was the concept of *dharma* on the human plane, and *rita* on the cosmic plane.

Dharma in the Mahabharata

The concept of *dharma* in practice has more than one meaning and so is not considered easy to understand. The *Mahabaharata* explains this in a number of ways.[3] In a general way *dharma* means prescriptions, the observance of which keeps human beings from falling from the station of life or from their own true selves. This is what Sri Krishna says in the *Mahabharata*. Adherence to *dharma* protects men from evils created by men. According to Mookerjee, *dharma* can have two derivations from the Sanskrit. In the first, *dharma* is a means to attain *dhana*, that is, value, both material and spiritual. By the second derivation it means that which preserves creation and protects it from harm and bestows good. In the second sense *dharma* is the law of both human and non-human existence, the *rita* in the Riga Veda. The prescriptions of the *dharmashastras* define *dharma* in the human situation, for man's material and spiritual good. *Dharma* prescribes actions leading to the achievement of *artha* (the economic good) and *kama* (the hedonistic good). *Dharma* with *artha* and *kama* is called the *trivarga* and is prescribed for a householder. By artha is meant riches, might, skill, family health, fame, and enjoyable objects. *Kama* is enjoyment itself; it is desire for pleasure. To achieve *artha* and *kama* by means other than the prescribed *dharma* is to commit a wrong—that is, sin. To acquire them in the prescribed way is good—that is, to acquire merit.

Regarding the relative merit of *dharma*, *artha*, *kama* and *moksha*, there is a dialogue among Vidura and the five Pandava(s) in the *Mahabharata*.[4] Yudhisthira opened the dialogue by saying that with *dharma*, *artha*, and *kama* is carried out our daily life. Of these three, which is superior to which? To this Vidura said that learning, asceticism and meditation, forgiveness, simplicity, kindness, truthfulness, and restraint are the elements of *dharma*. Taken severally, *dharma* is the highest value. *Artha* is subservient to *dharma*. *Kama*, taken by itself, is inferior to the other two. Then Arjuna said that *artha* is the principal value because it is the aid to *karma*, to the pursuits of life like faming, trade, dairy, industry, etc. With *artha* one can achieve enjoyable objects in life and can perform the prescriptions of *dharma* in a better way. Also the motivation to acquire *artha* is very strong in man. Nakula and Sahadeva were of the view that *dharma* and *artha* should go together. Adhering to *dharma* and earning *artha* without transgressing *dharma* was the best way. It will then be like nectar mixed with honey. With *dharma-artha* one should go for enjoyment of life. Bhimasena's answer was a notable one. He said *kama* or desire is the driving force of life. It is by desire for the pleasures of heaven that great sages are motivated and are engaged in religious performances, austerity, etc. It is by desire that the trader, the farmer, artists, and artisans are engaged in their respective professions. *Kama* is the essence even in all our prescribed behaviours and our efforts at earning riches, fame, etc. *Dharma* and *artha*, that is, virtue and riches, are useless without *kama*. But it is best to pursue the *trivarga*, the 'triple' value, that is, *dharma-artha-kama*. To pursure only one of them is worst, two only better.

Yudhisthira spoke last. *Moksha* is the highest value, he said. One should do the duities of his station of life without any self-seeking. This is practising *dharma* with indifference to sin or merit, riches or poverty, pleasure or plain.

In the above dialogue, *dharma* has many meanings: As the highest value, as subject to *artha*, as being bound to *artha*, as being subject to desire, as being subject to *moksha*, or liberation.

Bhishma later on also told the Pandavas in the *Mahabharata* that *moksha* is the highest value for man. Quoting ancient tales, he told them that both pain and pleasure are transitory, one following the other in a causal cycle driven by presisting desire. Of the two—happiness gained by effort driven by desire and happiness gained by forsaking desire—the latter is preferable because it frees man from the cycle of pleasure and pain.

But though *moksha* or liberation was considered by Bhishma as the supreme aim of life, the way to it for a king was through the following of *dharma*. The king was bound by *dharma* and anything he commanded had to be according to law. As a matter of *dharma*, a king had to look to the welfare of his subjects, secure the kingdom from external attack, keep men to their stations of duty, decide carefully on war and peace, maintain a well-trained army and efficient police and intelligence services. So long as one remains a king he should follow the *trivarga* guided by *dharma*, not by *kama* as Bhimasena had said, like an ideal householder. Bhishma also enumerated the personal qualities that a king should have, like earning riches without cruelty, being brave without being a braggart, etc., and the qualities that a king must not have, such as showing charity to the greedy, trusting a man of ill will, indulgence in sex, etc. The king should also be a shrewd ruler and put up a show when necessary like an actor. Pretension of friendship with a strong enemy and at the same time preparing secretly for war at an opportune moment against him was a valuable piece of advice that Bhishma gave Yudhisthira as a matter of *dharma*. Bhishma also gave such advice as abjuration of anger, adherence to truth, proper distribution of wealth, forgiveness, having children by one's own wife, purity of thought and action, non-violence, simplicity, and care for the dependents—the ninefold *dharma*. During the war, Sri Krishna told Arjuna that non-violence is a great *dharma* and that telling a lie is preferable to violence. This sounds contradictory in view of Sri Krishna's advice to Arjuna in the *Bhagavad Gita* to engage in the war. In this context, Sri Krishna's reply to Sanjaya, Dhritarashtra's envoy to Yudhisthira just before the war broke out, is quite interesting.

Sanjaya, trying to dissuade Yudhisthira from war in the name of *dharma*, said that one who takes *dharma* as superior to *kama* and *artha* is great. Desire for *artha* binds one to sorrow. Therefore, Yudhisthira, the champion of *dharma*, had better live by begging than killing such men as Drona, Asvatthama, Kripa, Salya, Vikarna, Duryodhana, Karna. War is evil, desire is a blemish on the pious soul. That war has no necessary connection with virtue or vice, but that war is unmitigated evil is evident from the fact that a senseless fellow or a sinner may win wealth by war, while the sensible and virtuous may lose. To this Sri Krishna replied that no one could abandon his station of duty. One must act, and act according to the injunctions and prescriptions of *dharma*. Knowledge for the sake of knowledge is really empty; it must guide action. The whole universe is in activity without respite, nothing is at rest. Indra is the king of gods because he is untiring in his care and concern for them and sticks to truth and *dharma*, looking to others before looking into his own happiness. Yudhisthira being a king was duty bound to wage war to reclaim his birth-right, the kingdom that had been fraudulently taken away from him. This was his bounden duty, his *dharma*.

Dharma in the Ramayana

The notion of *dharma* is central in *Ramayana*. *Dharma*, coming from the root word meaning "to sustain", has wide ranges of application in the *Ramayana*. In the mythical universe peopled by the gods, demons, humans, animals, and forces of nature, cosmic harmony is sustained through the observance of the principle of non-interference by all the inhabitants of the universe. Within each realm, *dharma* stands for the sustaining principle of social harmony: proper behaviour determined by the intrinsic nature of the inhabitants themselves. The *Ramayana* teaches the proper action of men through its hero, Rama, who plays the roles of ideal son, husband, king, and friend in the epic. Sita plays the role of an ideal wife, while Bharata more than Rama exemplifies the role of an ideal brother.

The conflict between Ravana and Rama is a confrontation between forces that create cosmic and social disharmony and forces that maintain cosmic and social harmony. Cosmic harmony is maintained by the gods, who assume a superior status as guardians of a universe comprised of demons, humans, animals, and forces of nature. While cosmic harmony is established by the gods, social harmony is maintained by kings, who rule in exemplary fashion and maintain conditions necessary for the fulfillment of duties and obligations by their subjects.

It needs to be pointed out, however, that the *Ramayana* advocates a pluralistic world with diverse, but appropriate, codes of moral behaviour or *dharma* for the various beings. This creates a tension between the different *dharmas.*

The *Ramayana* resolves the tension between a pluralistic view of moral behaviour and the idea of a universal morality as follow: while cosmic and social harmony are achieved by each group of inhabitants functioning within its own realm, such harmony can be sustained only by exceptional leadership in each group. The exceptional quality stems from the ability of the leaders to conform not only to their group *dharma* but also to the demands of universal *dharma.* Rule by such "enlightened, exceptional leaders" alone guarantees social and cosmic harmony. Such leaders would respect the territorial rights of other groups in the world and would not violate each others' borders. The stress of the *Ramayana* is thus on the maintenance of peace in the universe through everyone following their own *dharma(s).*

As to what the duties and obligations of a king should be and how a king should behave, there is a long discourse on this in the first book of *Ramayana*. The context is the effort of Bharata to change the mind of Rama, so that he would end his exile and return to Ayodhya and assume the burden of kingship. Rama refuses on the ground that it would violate the solemn promise he had made to his father, and he begins to advice Bharata about how he should rule the kingdom of Ayodhya. As Sundarayan points out Rama gives his advice in the form of a series of questions that he poses to Bharata:

> Has the kingdom suffered from your youthful inexperience? Have you in service, for the tending of sacred fires, a brahmin who is versed in the traditions, intelligent and just? Have you overcome sleep? In the second half of the night do you reflect on the means to ensure success in your enterprise? Have you got counselors who are prudent, brave, skillful and perspicacious? Are your ministers incorruptible? Are the leaders of your army brave? Do the men and women live happily in your kingdom? Have you as a king eschewed the fourteen failings: Atheism, dissimulation, inattention, anger, procrastination, lack of discrimination in companionship, gratification of senses, disregard of counsel, consultation with those who advocate what is ill advised, failure to carry out what has been decided, disclosure of counsel received, omission of sacred practice in the early morning and desire to enter into combat with all thy foes at the same time?[5]

Ramayana depicts the kingdom ruled by Dasharatha, the father of Rama, as a model society. In his kingdom everyone practised his *varanadharama* (the caste duty), the men and women were of righteous conduct and self-controlled. The implication here is that if the king rules properly, the subjects will also behave properly and fulfill their duties and responsibilities. Hence, the primary responsibility of maintaining the proper functioning of society rests with the king and the royal house. A king has to maintain the highest standards of personal morality. He has to protect his subjects, and this duty requires vigilance on his part against the forces of evil and the forces of disruption both within his kingdom and outside it.

Kautilya's Arthashastra

The *Arthashastra* of Kautilya develops its State policy from the Vedas. In the Vedas, the great aims of human endeavour are *dharma, artha, kama* and *moksha*. Of these, *moksha* has always been held, unanimously and unambiguously, to be highest ideal to which a human being can aspire. It is not easy to define *moksha;* it is basically, self-realization through liberation—the liberation from earthly bondage by realizing the divine in the human, the spiritual in the physical and the *atman* or soul in the mind-body complex. It is the final beatific and timeless state of the enfranchized soul, and it is not possible to achieve it by mere mental processes or literary thought. However, the pursuit of the three objectives—*dharma, artha* and *kama*—can contribute to the attainment of *moksha*.

Of the three objectives capable of being studied and practised, *dharma* has always occupied the premier place. Dharma not only signifies an absolute and immutable concept of righteousness but also includes the idea of duty which every human being owes to oneself, to one's ancestors, to society as a whole and to universal order. *Dharma* is law in its widest sense—spiritual, moral, ethical and temporal. Every individual, whether the ruler or the ruled, is governed by his or her own *dharma*. To the extent that society respected *dharma*, it protected itself. This concept has been very much enlarged by the *dharmashastras* or the *smritis*. The literature on the *dharmashastras*, the original scriptures and the commentaries thereon, is very extensive. For our present purpose, we need only observe that everything in Vedic polity—the rights and duties of rulers, ministers, priests and people—is governed by the concept of *dharma*. According to the *Arthashastra*:

[The observance of] one's own *dharma* leads to heaven

> and eternal bliss. When *dharma* is transgressed, the resulting chaos leads to the extermination of this world. Whoever upholds his own *dharma*, adheres to the customs of the Aryas and follows the rules of the *varnas* and the stages of life, will find joy here and in the hereafter. For the world, when maintained in accordance with the Vedas, will ever prosper and not perish. Therefore, the king shall never allow the people to swerve from their *dharma* (1.3.14-17).[6]

In the *trivarga*, *artha*, (it is to be noted), follows *dharma* in the threefold objectives of life and thereafter leads to enjoyment, *kama*. As used by Kautilya in his treatise, the *Arthashastra*, *artha* has a much wider significance than merely 'wealth'. The material well-being of individuals is a part of it. As Kautilya says in the concluding section of his book: 'The source of livelihood of men is wealth'. He then draws the corollary that the wealth of a nation is both territory of a state and its inhabitants who may follow a variety of occupations (15.1.1).[7] The State or government has a crucial role to play in maintaining the material well-being of the nation and its people. Therefore, an important part of *Arthashastra* is 'the science of economics', including starting productive enterprises, taxation, revenue collection, budget and accounts.

As Kangle points out, with *artha* understood, by implication, in the sense of the earth where men live and seek their material well-being, it ceases to be the goal pursued by individuals and appears as the means of ensuring the well-being of men in general. The extension of meaning makes it possible for *Arthashastra* to be regarded as the *shastra*, or treatise, concerned with general well-being on earth. And since State activity alone can make such general well-being possible, the protection of the earth and its acquisition, which are an essential part of State activity, are declared to be the province of this *shastra*. It is thus defined as the *shastra* which shows how this activity of the acquisition and protection of the earth should be carried out.

This definition implies that *Arthashastra* has a twofold

aim. First, it seeks to show how the ruler should protect his territory. This protection refers principally to the administration of the State, to its domestic policy. Secondly, it shows how territory should be acquired. This acquistion refers principally to the conquest of territory from others; that involves a consideration of the foreign policy of the State. These two cover the whole range of State activity. One may say, therefore, that *Arthashastra* is to be understood as the science dealing with State affairs in the internal as well as the external sphere; in other words, it is the science of statecraft or of politics and administration.[8]

Since the aim of administration is the promotion of the welfare of the subjects, the State is required to have an economic policy. One of the aims of pursuing successful economic policies, particularly through productive enterprises, is also to increase the revenues of the State and appropriate the surpluses for the State treasury. *Kosha* (treasury) is an essential constitutent of the State. 'A King with a depleted treasury eats into the very vitality of the citizens and the country' says Kautilya (2.1.16). At the same time, a King who impoverishes his own people or angers them by unjust exactions will also lose their loyalty (7.5.27). A balance has to be maintained between the welfare of the people and the need for augmenting the resources of the State.[9]

The welfare of the people presuposes two things—maintenance of law and order and an adequate administrative machinery. In this context, maintaining law and order involves not only the detection and punishment of criminals but also upholding the fabric of society. According to Kautilya, the State has a responsibility for ensuring the observance of laws concerning relations between different sections of society and other similar civil matters. Further, there have to be laws to avoid losses to the State treasury and to prevent embezzlement or misuse of power by servants of the State.

The extensive responsibilities of the State for promoting economic well-being and preserving law and order demand an equally extensive administrative machinery. Kautilya's

Arthashastra contains details of the organisation of the civil service. as well as the duties and responsibilities of individual officials.

Kautilya elaborates on the need for State regulation. He states in the *Arthashastra:*

> When people were oppressed by the law of the fishes (*matsyanyaya*, according to which the bigger fish swallow the smaller ones), they made Manu, the son of Vivasvat, the king. They fixed one-sixth part of the grains and one-tenth of their goods and money as his share. Kings who receive this share are able to ensure the well-being of their subjects (1.13.5-7).

As Kangle remarks on the above verse, here is the *raison d'etre* for regulation by the State. The original state of nature is imagined to be one of total anarchy, where might alone was right. People agree to pay taxes and to be ruled by a king in order that they may be able to enjoy security and well-being. This makes for a mutually beneficial interaction between the State and the citizens.[10]

The duty of the ruler to protect his subjects implies something more than mere protection of person and property. It also implies *yogakshema*. As is well-known, yoga refers to the successful accomplishment of an object, while *kshema* refers to the peaceful, undisturbed enjoyment of that object. Security, that is, protection by the State is essential for both. But ensuring the two, means something more than merely providing security. In fact, *yogakshema* implies the idea of welfare, well-being, including the idea of prosperity, happiness, and so on.

There is another aspect of the protection which is laid down as the ruler's duty. Protection also implies, as already mentioned, the protection of the social order founded on the system of *varnas* and *ashramas*. The ruler is asked to see that every one carries out the duties of the *varna* or *ashrama* to which he belongs as laid down in the *trayidharma* or the Vedic way. The preservation of the Vedic social order is thus a duty laid on the ruler. Consequently, it can be said that the State has to maintain

Vedic *dharma*. That, however, does not means that a theological State is being thought of. No organized theological body was there to intervene in the affairs of the State to safeguard religious interests or to enforce religious sanctions.

The protection of the subjects is to be done with the help of *danda*,[11] force of punishment, which is the symbol of the ruler's authority. With the help of *danda* the ruler is to maintain peace and order in the realm so that wealth and prosperity may increase. Therefore, an integral part of *Arthashastra* is *dandaniti*, the enforcement of laws by a voluminous and comprehensive set of fines and punishments.[12]

A ruler's duties in the internal administration of the country are said by Kautilya to be three-fold: *raksha* or protection of the state from external aggression, *palana* or maintenance of law and order within the state, and *yogakshema* or safeguarding the welfare of the people.

The prosperity of the State and its inhabitants cannot be increased unless new territory is acquired by settlement of virgin lands, by alliance or by conquest. In a political environment which had many kings, any one of them resting content with his own territory was likely to fall prey to the expansionist ambitions of another. How to deal with other kings by using peaceful or warlike methods is the foreign policy aspect of acquisition (*labha*) of new territory, and so preparing for, and waging war, also becomes an integral part of the science of governance in addition to the use of diplomatic means.

Kautilya's System of Economic Administration[13]

Kautilya's *Arthashastra* is one of the world's oldest treatises on the economic administration of a State. The aim of the three main types of economic activity of the time, namely, agriculture, cattle rearing and trade, was to generate resources in the form of grains, cattle, gold, forest produce and labour. Using these, the king obtained a treasury and an army, which were then used to bring under his control both his own people and the people of the enemy (1.4.1, 2). Wealth alone enabled the creation of more wealth (9.4.27), while a king with a depleted treasury ate into the very vitality of the country (2.1.16).

The wealth of the State was the totality of the surplus stored in the King's treasury, the commodity warehouse, the granary, the store for forest produce and the ordnance depots (2.5.1). Of these, the treasury was the most important; the king is advised to devote his best attention to it, because all the activities of the State depended on it (2.8.1,2). In the order of importance of the six internal constituents of the State, the treasury is placed immediately below the king and ministers (the State apparatus) and the people, both rural and urban. The treasury is ranked above the army because 'the army is dependent on finance; in the absence of resources, a (disaffected) army goes over to the enemy or even kills the king' (8.1.47,48).

The accumulation of wealth by the State was made possible by the fact that the king was the principal and residual owner of all property. All land in the country not specifically owned by an individual was State property. All water belonged to the king and users paid a water rate for taking water from irrigation works built by the State (2.24.18). irrespective of whether the cost of building a dam or an embankment was born entirely or only partly by the State, all the fish, ducks and green vegetables produced in or near the reservoirs were the king's property (2.1.24). When there was a dispute about the ownership of a field or a pasture and neither claimant succeeded in providing his title to it, the property reverted to the king. If the owner of a property disappeared, the king became the owner (3.9.17). When a man died without heirs, the king inherited his property, except for the amounts needed for the funeral and the maintenance of the widow (3.5.28). In any auction, either of immovable property by individuals (3.9.3-6) or of goods by foreign traders at city gates (2.21.7-9), the difference between the price fixed by the seller and the price actually realized by the auction, was deposited in the treasury of the State.

The *Arthashastra* also delineates what the ruler, or the

State has to do for the welfare of the subjects. The ruler is to undertake such activities as settlement on virgin land, building of dams, tanks and other irrigation works, providing pastures for cattle, opening trade-routes and ensuring safety on them, working of mines, and so on.

The ruler having to allow the interests of the subjects to prevail over those of the State, it is laid down that the sale of commodities, whether indigenous or imported, should be arranged in such a way that the subjects are benefitted thereby and that any profit that may be harmful to the subjects is avoided. Further it is said that when the subjects are struck down by natural calamities, the ruler should take care of them like a father. The ideal set before the ruler is that of paternalistic rule.

The intervention of the State in the economic system was to be a limited though essential one. The State had, for example, no distributive or equity functions which are supposed to be performed by individuals considering the interests of others, whether in one's own society or in other societies, as a part of their *dharma* and in their drive for liberation. The stress is on the individual who has to labour for his livelihood for the "gods befriend none but him who has laboured".[14] He has to perform all action in a spirit of service and consecrate it to the Lord. This attitude and the fact that his ultimate objective is liberation makes him keep only as much of his earnings and wealth as he needs keeping in mind the Vedic injunction of "not being greedy".[15] This makes him a trustee (on behalf of God) rather than an owner of wealth. There are thus no property rights in the manner in which they exist in modern capitalist societies, that is, as an absolute right without any corresponding responsibilities.

The main guiding principles of the administration of the economy were that the State should run a diversified economy actively, efficiently, prudently and profitably. The king was advised to maintain a diversified economy, within the limits of the technology available at that time, as follows: keep in good repair existing productive forests, elephant forests, reservoirs or mines; start new mines, factories, forests, elephant forests and cattle herds; promote trade and commerce by setting up market towns, ports and trade routes; build storage reservoirs; and organize new settlements (2.1.19.20).

The king is advised to be ever active in the management of the economy because the root of wealth is economic activity; inactivity brings material distress. Without an active policy, both current prosperity and future gains are destroyed (1.19.35, 36). Efficient management was therefore encouraged. Any official who did not generate adequate profits in a Crown undertaking was punished for 'swallowing the labour of workers' (2.9.17).

The State and private merchants, both local and foreign, were involved in trade. The Chief Controller of State Trading was responsible for the equitable distribution of local and foreign goods, buffer stocking, sale of Crown commodities and public distribution. He could appoint private traders as agents for the sale, at fixed prices, of Crown commodities or sell them direct to the public through state-owned retail outlets (2.16.8, 14-16). A crucial injunction regarding trade with foreign countries given to the Cheif Controller of State Trading was: 'Generate profits; avoid losses.' (2.16.25) The regulations for buffer stocks and futures emphasized profitability (2.16.2, 3: 4.2.36). When Crown commodities were sold by private merchants, they had to pay a charge to compensate the State for the profit which it would otherwise have got by selling direct (2.16.9).

Most of the productive economic activity took place in the *janapada* or villages with clearly marked boundaries. 'Power comes from the countryside, which is the source of all activities.' (7.14.19). An ideal *janapada* was one which was easily defended and which had a lot of productive land with cultivable fields, mines, timber forests, elephant forests and pastures. It should be capable of producing a wide variety of commodities, thus supporting the native population as well as outsiders who might immigrate in times of trouble. It should be rich enough to support a high level of taxation and a large army. Its people should be predominantly agricullturists, artisans and craftsmen, devoted to work, honest, loyal and intelligent (6.1.8).

Agriculture was considered the most important economic activity. 'Cultivable land is better than mines because mines fill only the treasury while agricultural production fills both the treasury and the storehouses.' (7.11.10-12). The king had to ensure that agriculturists were protected from harassment by not levying enormous taxes or fines and by not making undue demands for free labour (2.1.37). Other kinds of economic activities were: building forts (i.e., defence preparedness) so as to ensure a haven for the king and the people in times of trouble; water works and reservoirs as the source of crops; trade routes as the means of outmaneouvering the enemy, because through them the king could send secret agents and bring in weapons and other war material; mines as the source of war material; productive forests for providing material for building forts, carriages and chariots; elephant forests for capturing elephants; and animal herds for providing cattle, horses, donkeys and camels (7.14.21, 23-25).

Availability of water was important. In Kautilya's view it was better to acquire a smaller tract of land with flowing water than a larger but drier one (7.11.3). Among forests, one watered by a river was better because it was self-sustaining and provided shelter in times of calamities (7.12.7). It was necessary to build storage reservoirs becaue the water stored after a good rainfall could be made available continuously for irrigation (7.14.21,22). A dam built to impound the water of a flowing river was better than a reservoir to which water had to be brought by man-made canals. When damming rivers, preference was to be given to one which irrigated a larger area (7.12.4,5).

The organization of new settlements in uninhabited but cultivable areas of the country was an important activity of the State, not only for the increased revenue it would bring but also to make the country more easily defendable. Even in time of great financial stringency,the king was advised to promote new settlements by grants of grain, cattle and money (5.2.4). The settlements needed to be populated mainly by the three lower *varnas* becauseof the variety of benefits these provided.'Farmers are dependable and productive; cowherds make agriculture and othe activities possible by opening up pasture lands; and rich traders are a source of goods and money' (7.11.21). Though generally officials were paid partly in cash and partly by grant of land, Kautilya, recommends that, in new settlements, all salaries should be paid only in cash and no land allotted until the new village had fully stablized (5.3.32).

Kautilya gives is great detail how the State should look after the economy. But it is noteworthy that the role of the State, though crucial, is limited to a few things—law and order, light taxes, and ensuring the welfare of the people. The role was such as to allow each individual to find self-fulfilment and happiness for, in the ultimate analysis, in their happiness and welfare was the happiness of the king.

Dharmashastras and the State's Duties

Both Kautilya's *Arthashastra* and *Manusmriti* deal with the duties of the king. The *Arthashastra* has many regulations concerning the king. The foremost is that he has to look after the welfare of his subjects. As Kautilya says:

> In the happiness of his subjects lies the king's happiness; in their welfare his welfare. He shall not consider as good only that which pleases him but treat as beneficial to him whatever pleases his subjects (1.19.34).[16]

The king should not only obey his own *rajadharma* but also ensure that his subjects obeyed their respective *dharma(s)*. For. 'when *adharma* overwhelms *dharma*, the king himself will be destroyed' (3.16.42). Hence, a wicked prince, who hates *dharma* and is full of evil, should not be installed on the throne, even if he is an only son (1.17.51). In fact, Kautilya prefers an ignorant king who had not been taught *dharma* to a wicked king who, in spite of his learning, deviates from it (8.2.12).

The king's own *dharma* is to be just, impartial and lenient in protecting his people (8.2f.12). The king's attitude to his people should be like that of a father towards his children, particaularly when any danger threatened the population (4.3.43). He should treat leniently, like a father, those in new settlements whose tax exemptions had ceased to be effective (2.1.18).

No doubt there was an element of self preservation in this. Discontented and impoverished people might be provoked to revolt; they may then kill their king or go over to the enemy (7.5.27). The king should not tax the people unjustly because 'that will make the people angry and spoil the very sources of revenue' (5.2.70). A weak king who needed to recoup his depleted strength should try to promote the welfare of his people so that he might have the support of the countryside (7.14.18).

The king is expected to be well trained (3.1) and practise self-control (3.2). An ideal king is one who has the highest qualities of leadership, intellect, energy and personal attributes (6.1.2-6) and behaves like a sage monarch, a *rajarishi*. Among other things, a *rajarishi* is one 'who is ever active in promoting the welfare of the people and who endears himself to his people by enriching them and doing good to them' (1.7.1).

The *Manusmriti* or the Manu *dharmashastra* deal with *dharma* in its broadest sense. According to Manu, the concept of *dharma* gets diluted as we go from the Golden Age to the other ages. Says Manu (1.81,82):

> In the Golden Age, *Dharma* is four-footed and entire, and (so is) Truth; nor does any gain accrue to men by unrighteousness.
>
> In the other (three ages), by reason of (unjust) gains, *Dharma* is deprived sucessively of one foot, and through (the prevalence of) theft, falsehood, and fraud the merit (gained by men) is diminished by one-fourth (in each).

Manu also lays down the six measures of State policy concerning hostilities as alliance, war, marching, halting, dividing the army, and seeking protection (7.160). He then goes on to delineate the four expedients of politics as so arranging matters that neither friends, nor neutrals, nor foes are superior to oneself. The State has also to fully consider the future and immediate results of all actions (7.177,178).

According to Manu, the first and foremost duty of the king (State) is said to be the protection of his subjects and the ensuring of their well-being and welfare. He can only collect legally imposed taxes after he has protected those engaged in economic activity.[17] He has also to ensure the continuance of the societal structure as represented by the *varnashrama* system.[18] Moreover, he has to protect the people from anti-social elements like deceitful manufacturers and traders.

Manu also requires the ruler to learn the theory of various trades and professions.[19] The ruler has to collect taxes to enable him to conduct the affairs of State. But the amount of tax that a king can collect is very rigidly regulated. According to Manu:

> After (due) consideration the king shall always fix in his realm the duties and taxes in such a manner that both he himself and the man who does the work receive (their due) reward.
>
> As the leech, the calf, and the bee take their food little by little, even so must the king draw from his realm moderate annual taxes.
>
> A fiftieth part of (the increments on) cattle and gold may be taken by the king, and the eighth, sixth, or twelfth part of the crops.
>
> He may also take the sixth part of trees, meat, honey, clarified butter, perfumes, (medical) herbs, substances used for flavouring food, flowers, roots, and fruit;
>
> Of leaves, pot-herbs, grass, (objects) made of cane, skins, of earthen vessels, and all (articles) made of stone.[20]

Manu specifically warns the ruler to follow the middle path in levying taxes—neither too little nor too much.

> Let him not cut put his own root (by levying no taxes) nor the root of other (men) by excessive greed; for by cutting up his own root (or theirs), he makes himself or them wretched.[21]

Manu goes on to detail the qualities necessary for a king to be able to function in an optimal manner. He has to be truthful, act after due consideration and not be overly fond of sense enjoyments.

> They declare that king to be a just inflicter of punishment, who is truthful, who acts after due consideration, who is wise, and who knows (the respective value of) virtue, pleasure, and wealth (*dharma, kama* and *artha*).
>
> A king who properly inflicts (punishment), prospers with respect to (those) three (means of happiness); but he who is voluptuous, partial, and deceitful will be destroyed even through the (unjust) punishment (which he inflicts).[22]

Also he has to be pure, follow the *dharmashastras* and be just, modest and humble.

> By him who is pure (and) faithful to his promise, who acts according to the Institutes (of the sacred law), who has good assistants and is wise, punishment can be (justly) inflicted.
>
> Let him act with justice in his own domain, with rigour chastise his enemies, behave without duplicity towards his friend, and be lenient towards brahmins.
>
> The fame of a king who behaves thus, even though he subsists by gleaning, is spread in the world, like a drop of oil on water.
>
> Let him, though he may already be modest, constantly learn modesty from them; for a king who is modest never perishes.[23]

Manu also stresses the need for the king to conquer his senses and acquire knowledge.

> From those versed in the three Vedas let him learn the threefold (sacred science), the primeval science of

government, the science of dialectics, and the knowledge of the (supreme) Soul; from the people (the theory of) the (various) trades and professions.

Day and night he must strenuously exert himself to conquer his senses; for he (alone) who has conquered his own senses, can keep his subjects in obedience.[24]

Both Manu and Kautilya stress the need for the king to be a *rajarishi* as that is the only way that the State can prosper. The king has to be constantly active in promoting the welfare of his subjects. Kautilya also gives in great detail all that is necessary for economic growth and development—an austere king, devoted ministers and honest executives. On the basis of what Manu and Kautilya say it is possible to understand the underlying philosophy or concept on which their prescriptions are based. This philosophy is rooted in the Vedas. Discussed in the following paras is this Vedic thought and its link with the administrative prescriptions of the *dharmashastras*.

Vedic Administrative Philosophy

The concept of administration, in Vedic thought, has to vary according to the nature of the State and society. It will be one type in a feudal set up, another in a totalitarian one, and still another in a democratic one. The philosophy of Vedic administration, as we have seen, has to be derived from the inalienable dignity and worth of the human personality and the active concern that the State has to exhibit to foster the same. Its operative principle is that man is essentially educable and not vile, and that social change is, and can be, brought about in an orderly way and peacefully.

The *dharmashastras* give us profound insights into such a philosophy and its relevance to all men of responsibility, into which category fall all managers and administrators. Philosophy is like a lamp, it illumines the way. A single person needs only a small lamp to light his way. But a large congregation will need a more powerful light to light its way. Similarly, an ordinary philosophy is enough to light the path of a private citizen. But a more-than-ordinary philosophy is necessary to light the path of life and work of a man of social responsibility. What is the nature and scope of this more-than-ordinary philosophy?

In his brief but masterly introduction in his commentary on the *Bhagavad Gita*. Shankaracharya conveys in two sentences the nature and scope of this philosophy;

> 'The Vedanta (culmination of the Vedas) is (an integrated philosophy of a twofold *dharma*, namely, *pravritti* or outward-directed action and *nivritti* or inward-directed meditiation, which (together) form the means for the maintènance of the world on an even keel: for they are, verily, the means of the *abhyudaya*, social welfare, and *nihshreyasa*, spiritual growth and fulfilment, of all beings'.[25]

Philosophy is seeing life steadily and seeing it as a whole. Politics, economics, sociology, art, ethics, and religion view life in segments, and they thus form parts of the science of man. Similarly physics, chemistry, and biology view nature in segment, and form parts of the science of physical nature. But the philosophy, or *brahmavidya*, of the Veda, is the science of sciences being the synthesis of the sciences of physical nature and the sciences of human nature.

It is in the light of this *brahmavidya* that the Vedic philosophy of management is established. This philosophy calls for an integrated approach such that every person in the organization can fulfil himself. Great stress is laid on the behaviour of those who form the top management. Their job is to lead by example, to trust others, to enable everyone to find happiness and bliss. The concept is that of leaders imbued with the concepts of the Vedic seers, the *rishis*.

Kautilya's *Arthashastra* therefore calls for the king being a *rajarishi*. This word evokes all sorts of distorted meanings, magical and misty. We have to remove all such distorted meanings from our minds: And then we shall find a wonderfully constructive and creative idea in it. Shankaracharya defines this word as-'they who are both *rajas* (kings) and *rishis* (sages) in one.' What does that mean? We very few *rajas* in the sense of kings or crowned heads today. There are thus no *rajas* in the formal sense of the term, in the sense arising from the external accoutrements attched to the office of a *raja*. Who, then, is a *raja* in its essential sense? Anyone on whom depends the happiness and welfare of thousands. This is the meaning of the word *raja* in the Sanskrit tradition, the one who shines in responsibility. In this sense, the administrator is a *raja*; a manager is a *raja*; an industrial magnate is a *raja*; for, on them depend the happiness and welfare of thousands.

The combination of a *raja* and a *rishi* in an administrator, the synthesis of manliness and saintliness, this is what is desired by the Veda. When one combines power and social responsibility with the strength arising from character, clear thinking, dedication, and practial efficiency, one effects in oneslf this unique synthesis of the *rajarishi*. So Sri Krishna says in the opening three verses of the fourth chapter of the *Bhagavad Gita*.

> I taught this immortal yoga to Vivaswan; he taught it to Manu who, in turn, taught it to Ikshvaku. Coming down thus in a tradition, this yoga was known to the *rajarishis*; in the course of long ages, this yoga was lost, O Arjuna. This same ancient yoga, this invaluable mystery, I am now imparting to you, finding in you a devotee and a friend.

Why was this yoga lost in the course of ages? asks Shankara in his commentary and answers; 'Because it fell into the hands of physical and mental weaklings and of those without discipline and control over their sense organs' and he adds that Sri Krishna taught it to men of high responsibility 'in order to strengthen them and, endowed with which, they may work successfully to protect and cherish the people.'

In this philosophy, there is the confluence of two energy steams, namely, the energy of vision and the energy of practical implementation, the energy of meditation and the energy of action. It signifies the confluence of the energy of Sri Krishna, the unarmed charioteer and the master of yoga, and the energy of Arjuna, fully armed for heroic action under the guidance of Sri Krishna.

This is the concept of efficient and effective action emerging from the philosophy of yoga of the *Bhagavsad Gita* and from its *rajarishi* spirit inspiring politics and administration. This is the meaning and significance of the grand testament of the *Bhagavad Gita* given in its closing verse,

> 'Where (there is) Sri Krishna, the master of yoga (and) where (there is) Partha, the wielder of the bow, there (in that society), I think, wealth, victory, welfare, and unshakable justice (shall prevail).'

The next chapter explores what this stress on yoga in the *Bhagavad Gita* signifies for management.

REFERENCES

1. Mahabharata quoted in R.P. Kangle, *The Kautiliya Arthashastra* (Delhi; Motilal Banarsidas, 1992), Vol. III, p. 5.
2. Cf. *Bhagavad Gita*, 3. 10. 11.

   "Having created mankind in the beginning together with *yagya*, the Creator said: By this shall you propagate. this shall be the milch cow of your desires.

   Cherish the *devas* with this; and may those devas cherish you, thus cherishing one another you shall reap the supreme good."
3. What follows is based on A. K. Mookerjee,"Dharma as the Goal; The Mahabharata" in *Hindu Spirituality*, ed. K. Sivaraman (Delhi; Motilal Banarsidas, 1995) pp. 1227-50.
4. Mookerjee, *ibid.*, pp. 136-37.
5. K.R. Sunderayan, "The Ideal of the Perfect Life: The Ramayana," in *Hindu Spirituality*, note 3, p. 114.
6. L. N. Rangarajan, *Kautilya: The Arthashastra* (New Delhi: Penguin, 1995), pp. 107-8.
7. *Ibid.*, p. 100.
8. Kangle, note ' p. 2.

9. Rangarajan, note 6.
10. Kangle, note 1, p. 116.
11. The *danda* means rod or staff.
12. See Kangle, note 1, pp. 118-20.
13. All quotations are from Rangarajan, note 6, unless otherwise stated.
14. Rig Veda, 4.33.11.
15. Isha Upanishad, 1,
16. Rangarajan, note 6, p. x.
17. *Laws of Manu*, tr. by G. Buhler, 10.119. Hereinafter will be referred to as Manu.
18. *Ibid.*, 7.35.
19. *Ibid.*, note 3, 7.43.
20. *Ibid.*, 7. 128-32.
21. *Ibid.*, 7.139.
22. *Ibid.*, 7.26, 27.
23. *Ibid.*, 7.31-33, 39.
24. *Ibid.*, 7.43, 44.
25. Quoted by Swami Ranganathananda in *Democratic Administration in the Light of Practical Vedante* (Madras: Ramakrishna Mission, 1996), p. 45.

6

THE YOGIC MANAGEMENT OF THE BHAGAVAD GITA

The relatively outward-looking Vedas, and the inward-looking Upanishads, have been synthesized in the *Bhagavad Gita* whereby the inward-looking mystic has to be also the man of affairs. Such a synthesis would satisfy the modern need of having inner serenity while being actively involved in the affairs of the world. This is the way to steer oneself through the vicissitudes of the fast paced modern life and learn how to manage.

The setting of the *Bhagavad Gita* is the battlefield where a dialogue takes place between Sri Krishna and Arjuna. Arjuna, a young prince is the one who typifies in his own figure the man who seeks peace of mind amid worldly harassments, as well as the aspirant desirous of spiritual light. However, not until he is critically placed on a battlefield to fight against his beloved relatives, whom he sees confronting him in the opposing army, does he vehemently cry out for an answer to his questions. The battlefield, obviously, represents the battlefield of life in which we are placed in all kinds of circumstances whether we like them or not.

Arjuna, the disciple cries out for guidance. Only when his anguish becomes almost unbearable and his heart is deeply torn does the teacher, who is symbolized by the figure of the god-man Sri Krishna, appear.

Sri Krishna not only represents the embodied spiritual teacher, but he is ultimately the Divine within man, the God within who can illuminate all dark corners and answer all questions. He finds the disciple afflicted, agitated, and with eyes full of tears. He sees him perplexed with doubts, torn between the desire to do his duty in battle and the love for his relatives who oppose him in the enemy army. The occasion is used to give lengthy instruction upon spiritual subjects and techniques and how they relate to action in the world. At the end of the dialogue, after hearing all the teachings, the pupil's mind becomes peaceful. He says indeed: "My doubts are dispelled. Destroyed are my illusions. I will fight (act) (18.73)[1]."

The difficulties one meets in modern life can be met and managed after we gain such insight. Wisdom means ability to negotiate all the circumstances of life adequately, correctly, and with spiritual success. This understanding of the power lying latent within him becomes in time a man's anchor in the vicissitudes of life. He can ride the storms which life brings in the certainty that there is now something within him that they cannot shake from its position. The man of inspired life follows no iron law and clings to no rock-like plan. Sufficient for him to look within for right directon at all times and amidst all circumstances. To perceive the truth about any matter is to dispel all doubt. It also gives to action a tremendous ability to manage in a flexible manner and to adapt to the ever changing environment.

The deep spiritual comfort emanating from the teachings of the *Bhagavad Gita* is peculiarly needed at this stage of the world's affairs when everything is changing so rapidly and the human tendency is to cling to the known while the circumstances desire its destruction. The cry of Arjuna in the *Bhagavad Gita* could well be the lament of anyone who in today's world is asked to destroy the known.

Of what avail is dominion to us, O Teacher?

Of what avail are pleasures and even life?

> How can we be happy, after slaying our own people? Nay, I will not fight (2.8, 9).

The disciple is brought to the field of battle and told to fight. But he is confused with doubts. What is the use of it all, he asks? Who does not ask himself the same question in the stress and battle of our twentieth-century existence? Can one enter into the extreme competition of the business world, for instance, and still feel that he is not stifling his better instincts? Can he destroy systems or products which have been successful in the past and create new ones more suited to the changing tastes of consumers? Note how simply and understandingly this particular problem is answered by the teacher in the various verses that follow. The teacher says:

> For those who deserve no grief, thou hast grieved... Never did I not exist, nor thou, nor these rulers of men; and no one of us will ever hereafter cease to exist...Just as in this body the Self passes into childhood and youth and old age, just as one takes off old clothes and puts on new ones, so does he pass into another body...(2.11-13).

Here we have a dynamic principle which regards change as being good and natural. Chaos which follows the 'order' of today is the prelude to a higher and better order as new clothes come in place of the old ones which we throw away. Therefore, it is necessary to fight and to destroy, if necessary, that is, to act, to manage.

However, Arjuna looks at the teaching in a physical sense and not in its conceptual and dynamic managerial context. So there naturally comes to him the question: "Why should I act when all this is nothing but a dream? Where the very bodily existence is said to be no-existence? In such a situation, one thing is as good as another. Why shouldn't I retire and let others perform the action? Life is obviously a dream, therefore I will sit still and watch the dream go by."

This attitude, interestingly, indicates progress and is quite an advanced one at that. Why should one act when one does not want to act? Because, as the teacher points out, whatever you do you cannot refrain from acting. You cannot escape activity if you retreat from the world because you will still be involved in mental action. You may sit still and yet be held captive within the cycle of the finite, for you cannot escape from your thoughts. Your activity may change its character and become a mental one. But it is still activity.

The result is that you are no less bound to one than to the other. Meanwhile, the fact is that whether you act or sit still, so long as you are aware that you are in essence the Self, you are not caught up in the whirlpool of life. As you know that you cannot destroy the Self why should you be afraid of physical activity, of change, of both the known and the unknown? Go out into the world, do your duty, fight if need be, but act. Love and peace constitute your real nature and they do not change with your changing physical activities. Therefore, be inwardly the witness of life, as you wish to be, but do not be afraid of it. You cannot kill anyone, because you and they are ultimately both the same. Says the teacher:

> Thy concern is with action alone, never with results. Let not the fruit of action be thy motive, nor let thy attachment be for inaction. Steadfast in devotion do thy works, O Arjuna, casting off attachment, being the same in success and failure (2.47, 48).

Since you cannot escape activity, be it physical or mental, it follows that there is a path for the man of action, a way of managing life. The teacher then describes the path of action. He stresses the performance of duty and the repayment of the debt which one owes to one's own nature, to others, to society.

The real problem for the spiritual man is how to render efficient service and give himself up to his work in this feverish contemporary world and yet remain loyal to his inner call. The blissfulness of introspection may tempt him more and more to desert externals, but excessive introspection is only commendable in those whom destiny and duty have flung out of the world into monasteries and *ashramas* and retreats. For others the way is incessant work, as indeed the Lord Himself is constantly engaged in, so as to prevent the worlds from falling into chaos and destruction (3.24).

The *Bhagavad Gita* goes on to point out that work is a form of sacrifice. But as the teacher points out, it is a different kind of sacrifice than the one mentioned in the Vedas and the Upanishads. It is a sacrifice of service. It is necessary to serve because it is right to serve, to act because it is right to act, but sacrifice the result of your actions to destiny. This means that you do not act solely for reward. Do your work, perform your duty, not only for your personal need, but also with the idea of service. Do not concentrate only on results and personal benefits, but also work impersonally. This is the *Bhagavad Gita's* path of yoga, because it tends to curb desires and selfishness and helps to free one from bondage to the senses.

By acting in this way, say the *Bhagavad Gita*, the individual realizes that he is an adjunct of society, his life is social in nature and his own good and welfare lies in promoting the common weal. The more he contributes to social activity in a selfless way, the more society fulfills the necessities of his life. The *Bhagavad Gita's* idea of sacrifice, according to Sri Aurobindo, "contains in fact the eternal connecting truth of God and the world and works".[2] By effacing his selfish desire and in promoting the common interests of society, the individual sublimates his social life into a higher spiritual one. Sacrifice in the *Bhagavad Gita's* concept means exerting oneself for the benefit of others, in a word, service. And where service is rendered for service's sake, there is no room for attachment, likes and dislikes. Such a kind of selfless activity is not only a means for social welfare but also an end in itself, for it leads to social stability and growth of social solidarity.

From the viewpoint of society, sacrifice implies that society is organic by nature. Social life is interdependent, and the individual prospers not in isolation but living in communion with others. The *Bhagavad Gita* makes sacrifice socially-oriented, seeks to promote the integration of society on the one hand and the communitarian spirit of mutual service and sacrifice on the other. In other words, its concept implies that socio-economic growth and unity of society is more sacred and inviolable than the desire or quest for heavenly life for the individual.

The *Bhagavad Gita's* concept of *yagya* which envisages social unity, lays emphasis on desireless activity of the individual. While the Vedic thought considered religious activity as an end in itself, the Upanishads by the time of the *Bhagavad Gita* had come to be seen to emphasize knowledge and renunciation of activity. The *Bhagavad Gita* regarded both paths of activity as one-sided. To correct their limited outlook of activity, it drew the idea of activity from the Vedas and desirelessness from the Upanishads and synthesized the two—activity and desirelessness—into the yoga of desireless activity, which leads to the maintenance of the world in a state of unity through working for *lokasangraha* (welfare of the whole world).

Social Order of the Bhagavad Gita

The right to work of the *Bhagavad Gita*, which stands for the maintenance of society, is in need of the establishment of moral and political order. The *rita* of the Veda constitutes the moral law of the universe and governs it. The *Bhagavad Gita* transforms *rita* into *swadharma*[3] of the individual as the inviolable law of ethical life and activity.

Politically, the liberalism of the Bhagavad Gita is manifest in its concept of *swadharma*. Swadharma differs from person to person because of diversity in the natures of human beings. This implies that each individual is a distinct being, an end in himself with a distinct individuality of his own. The *swadharma* concept defends the dignity of the individual, his freedom, rights, obligations and encourages him to perfect his growth without external intervention.

The *Bhagavad Gita*, which as we have seen interprets Vedic terms like sacrifice in terms of social service, also aims at making practical the metaphysical concepts of the

Upanishads like the knowledge of the soul, renunciation and spiritual freedom by means of its concept of detached activity. It seeks to remove the barrier between the ideal of renunciation of secular activity by identifying the worldly pursuit of *dharma* with the selfless activity of the individual. It gives the utmost priority to the fulfillment of social and political obligations by the individual. According to it, even the man of realization has to perform them. It is this practical, activist path that distinguishes the *Bhagavad Gita* from the ascetic paths. While the ascetic ideal of renunciation of activity would provide us the concept of the spiritual individual who remains indifferent to society, the detached activity of the *Bhagavad Gita* makes social the nature and activity of such a spiritual individual.

The *Bhagavad Gita* accepts the Upanishadic concept of the soul and its attributes. According to the Upanishads, the desire for the knowledge of the soul is the beginning and its realization the end of the spiritual quest of the individual. As pointed out by Christopher Isherwood, "to seek to realize my essential nature is to admit that I am dissatisfied with my nature as it is at present."[4] By realizing the Atman or self, one sees the presence of Brahman or the universal self in all beings and things, and all in it.

As the soul is inherent in all beings, man is spiritual by nature. The individual, who strives for the realization of the self, tends to live alone. He is highly individualistic and intolerant of social intervention, which retards his spiritual growth. All the time he prefers to think and meditate on the knowledge of the self. But he who always looks within maintains no social nexus. He does not live for society, he is not of it and keeps aloof from it.

So while for the ascetic, the spiritual life of the individual and his secular activity stand apart from each other the same is not true in the yogic doctrine of the *Bhagavad Gita*. The *Bhagavad Gita* bridges the gulf between the individual self and the social self by means of its doctrine of detached activity, which is at once individual and social, spiritual and secular, in nature.

The *Bhagavad Gita* accepts the Upanishadic ideal of enjoyment through renunciation, of activity in a limited and conditional way. As in its attitude towards the Vedas, it corrects and expands the Upanishadic ideal. The watch-word of the Isha Upanishad "enjoy through renunciation," according to Swami Ranganathananda, "was later developed by the Gita into a comprehensive practical spirituality, in its theory of detached action."[5] Had Sri Krishna been convinced of the complete and perfect nature of the practice of renunciation of social activity, he could have permitted Arjuna to become a *sannyasi* or hermit on the battlefield itself. Instead he exhorts that what is to be renounced is not social and political activity but the fruit of desire itself while performing activity.

The *Bhagavad Gita* is of the view that the individual can seek freedom from ignorance, and the unhappiness and stress inherent in such ignorance, by practising detached activity. While the interested activity of the individual creates stress and strain, inactivity promotes dullness. Detached activity transcends the nature of egoistic activity as well as of inactivity. The spiritual growth and freedom of the individual becomes manifest here on earth itself by working with equanimity. Desireless action, can be interpreted in terms of Hegelian dialectics. Vedic activity in the world constitutes the thesis, Upanishadic inner activity the anti-thesis, and desireless action of the *Bhagavad Gita* the synthesis, which negates both the egoistic activity and renunciation of activity. There is a beginning and an end for thesis and anti-thesis, that is, for activity and renunciation, but desireless action is a continuous social and political process.

The social and political liberalism of the *Bhagavad Gita* becomes more pronounced when it adds social and political activity to the ideal of renunciation. The Upanishads declare that renunciation is the path for the realization of spiritual freedom by the individual. As against any uniform prescription, the method of the *Bhagavad Gita* is manifold. The *Bhagavad Gita*, which takes into consideration the diversity of human nature, the existing grade of social evolution and the present stage of spiritual growth of the individual, prescribes different methods of activity for different types of individuals in its system of the organization of the four-fold order of society. It is of the view that all kind of selfless activity lead to social and political growth and the realization of spiritual freedom. Selfless activity of one's calling is the concomitant of the spiritual freedom of the individual[6].

The *Bhagavad Gita* synthesizes and transforms the concept of the four orders of Vedic society through its doctrine of selfless activity. The *Bhagavad Gita* traces the concept of the four orders of society to the Vedic concept of psychological activity of the three *gunas* or qualities of nature (*sattva*, *rajas* and *tamas* or harmony, activity and inertia), which inhere in human nature and mould the functional duties of the different orders. The Purusha Sukta of the Rigveda, as we have seen, gives the first social expression to the division of society into the four classes. It speaks of an eternal sacrifice made by the cosmic *Purusha* which sustains man and the world. As the four classes sprang from the different parts of the cosmic *Purusha*, the class system in social terms symbolizes spiritual oneness and the organic character of society.

The *Bhagavad Gita* states that the four-fold caste order is eternal and universal in nature; it is a spiritual and social institution. The Supreme Being of the *Bhagavad Gita* avows: "The four orders of society (viz., the Brahmin, the Kshatriya, the Vaishya and the Shudra) were created by Me, classifying them according to their prenatal qualities and apportioning corresponding duties to them, (4.13)." The *Bhagavad Gita* (18.42-44) goes on to define the duties which inhere to the four castes:

> Calm, self-restraint, ascetic practice, purity,
>
> Long-suffering and uprightness,
>
> Wisdom in theory as in practice, religious faith,–
>
> (These) are the works of *Brahmins*, inhering in their nature.
>
> High courage, ardour, endurance, skill,

In battle unwillingness to flee,

An open hand, a lordly mien,–

(These) are the works of *Kshatriyas*, inhering in their nature (too).

To till the fields, protect the kine and to engage in trade,–

(These) are the works of *Vaishyas*, inhering in their nature;

But works whose very soul is service

Inhere in the very nature of the Shudra.

Sri Krishna's denial of hereditary birth as the basis of caste and his emphasis on quality and action for differentiating the functions gives to the social teaching of the *Bhagavad Gita* a significance and a progressive quality which is contrary to the conception of caste. He unleashes the creative forces of social liberalism in the caste order. He instills a new liberating faith in the individual that the pursuit of every caste-*dharma* embodies in itself functional equality, social freedom and spiritual growth. Sri Krishna proclaims that the individual could ascend from the lower to the higher caste, socially and spiritually, by improving and perfecting his caste-duty with dedication. He infuses a new life of synthesis into the social order by affirming the social dignity and individuality of every caste-duty in society.

Though the individual of the *Bhagavd Gita* embraces every aspect of social life, in its concept of the societal system, it is the ethical duty of the individual to seek the maintenance of society. It is the detached individual that has to lead and direct society and not vice versa. The individual therefore still remains paramount and his freedom is not constrained by society provided, of course, that he is detached and selfless.

One does not become social by merely living in society. The individual who lives in it must work for its unity and stability. The social nature of the individual, according to the *Bhagavad Gita*, finds fulfilment in the performance of selfless activity in a spirit of social oneness. It is the individual's instinct of the oneness of all beings that makes life social while social life is derived from the detached activity of the individual. It is by harmonisation of his social and individual duties that a person can play a proper role in society.

The Yoga of the Bhagavad Gita

The word yoga is derived from the root *yuj*, which means to unite or to join together, much like the etymological meaning of the word 'religion'. Yoga aims at the union of the human and the divine—all within oneself. It is a way to one's wholeness, an integration of all aspects and levels of oneself. One must not imagine that yoga is only a collection of certain practices devoid of a metaphysical basis. In fact, yoga is a perfectly structured and integrated world view aiming at the transformation of a human being from his actual and unrefined form to a perfected form. It can be said that yoga aims at freedom from nature, including freedom from human nature; its flight is to the transcendence of humanity and the cosmos, into pure being.

The classical text on yoga is Patanjali's *Yogasutra.*[7] According to the *Yogasutra* the purpose of yoga is to lead to silence of the mind (1.2). This silence is the prerequisite condition for the mind to be able to reflect accurately the objective reality without introducing its own subjective distortions. Yoga does not create this reality, which is above the mind, but only prepares the mind to apprehend it, by assisting in the transformation of the mind—from the ordinary mind full of noise, like a whole army of frenzied and drunken monkeys—to a still mind.

Even this transformation is not brought about by any effort or practice, as Patanjali's *Yogasutra* (4.2-3) reminds us, but is an unfolding of nature's own potential tendency. The practice and discipline of yoga are necessary only for removing the obstacles of this unfolding, just as a gardener removes the weeds for the sake of a healthy crop. Yoga attempts to eliminate the obstacles to the natural unfolding and development of the human being so that his or her true and real nature may be realized.

According to Patanjali the counterflow of the usual tendencies of the mind has to be attained through the eight limbs of yoga by steady practice (*abhyasa*) and increasing inwardness (*vairagya*). This is through the elaborated scheme of the eight limbs—*yama*, *niyama*, *asana*, *pranayama*, *pratyahara*, *dharana*, *dhyana*, and *samadhi*.

The first one, *yama*, refers to various self-restraints comprising abstention from violence, falsehood, theft, incontinence, and acquisitiveness.

The second limb, *niyama*, consists in the observances of purity, contentment, austerity, self study, and devotion to the Lord.

The third and fourth limbs, *asana* and *pranayama*, are concerned with the right posture, which makes one both relaxed and alert, and the proper regulation of breathing for steadying the attention.

The fifth limb, *pratyahara*, is the inward turning of the senses so that they can be freed of external impressions and come under the control of the purified mind.

The five limbs constitute the outer group out of the eight limbs of *Patanjali's* yoga, the other three being the inner limbs. *Dharana* is concentration in which the consciousness is bound to a single spot; *dhyana* is contemplation or meditative absorption in which there is an uninterrupted flow of attention from the observer to the observed. So far the observer has acted as the centre of consciousness which sees. When that centre is removed through the mind emptied of itself, that state is called *samadhi* (the *nirvana* of Buddhism), a state of silence, settled intelligence, and emptied mind, in which the mind becomes the object and reflects it truly, as it is.

The *Bhagavad Gita* expands the use of the word yoga enormously. In addition to the well-known yoga(s) called *karmayoga* (yoga of action), *bhakti-yoga* (yoga of love and devotion), *gyana yoga* (yoga of knowledge), *raja yoga* (another name for Patanjali's system) every chapter ends with a colophon labelling it a yoga. For example, the first chapter of the *Bhagavad Gita* ends with the colophon calling it "The Yoga of Arjuna's Confusion," and the eleventh chapter is called "The Yoga of the Vision of the Cosmic Form," and so on. Anything that can be made use of in the quest for the absolute and be harmonized with the general principles of yoga is called by it a specific sort of yoga.

Three further remarks can be parenthetically made here about the *Bhagavad Gita* since they are relevant to any discussion of yoga. First, the *Bhagavad Gita* is absolutely essential for an understanding of the system of yoga. Second, it extends the range and understanding of yoga at least in two different ways. By forging a link between the classical yoga of Patanjali and other metaphysical systems and metaphors, it enlarges our vision of the scope of yoga. By the whole, setting at the battlefield insistence on action in this world and the presence of Sri Krishna himself as a model Yogi, one is reminded that not only is there no conflict between work and the inner light but that rightly seen the outer action can and does serve the purpose of the inner light.

Third, the central yoga that Krishna teaches in the *Bhagavad Gits* is *buddhiyoga* (yoga of integrated intelligence and discernment) of which the various aspects are yoga (s) like *karmayoga*, *bhaktiyoga*, *jnanayoga*, *raja yoga*, etc. The place of *buddhi* in the *Bhagavad Gita* is central. Sri Krishna advises Arjuna to "seek refuge in *buddhi*" (2.49). He goes on to say, "To them who are constantly integrated worshipping me with love, I give that *buddhiyoga* by which they may draw near to me" (10.10). Later, during the process of summing up his entire teaching, Sri Krishna says again, "Renouncing mentally all actions to me, making me your goal, relying on *buddhiyoga*, become constantly mindful of me. Mindful of me, you will overcome all obstacles by my grace. But if because of self-centeredness you will not listen, you will perish" (18.57-58).

Buddhiyoga is very relevant to modern life since it implies the transcendence rather than the denial of ordinary rationality. Since the temper of modern times is suffused with rationality, the yoga of *Bhagavad Gita* enables the modern culture to retain its rational character and yet make contact wth genuine spirituality through the practice of *buddhiyoga*. This principle can be seen as operating in two ways. Modern life is characterized by activity. In such a context the call to *buddhi* as a means of probing the depths of the inner being and discovering the true nature of the universal individual can be a useful corrective to the cult of hyperactivity. But more generally:

> [*Buddhiyoga*] provides us with that rational procedure of self exceeding which forms the keynote of all human aspirations, whether they point to above or to below. Its rationale is to be found in the logical scheme of Sankhyan principles, where *buddhi* which forms the core of man's nature occupies a peculiar position which marks the farthest limit to which the concept of an upward march of evolutionary Nature can rise...[8]

Thus, the relevance of *buddiyoga* to life in the modern world arises out of its universal and universalizing potential.

Balance, Equality and Harmony

The yoga of the *Bhagavad Gita* also attempts to balance various aspects like relations between man and God, equality of the status between the individual and society, harmonious relations between man and man, and equality of ends and means.

Conceptually, the yogic ideal of maintaining balance or coexistence between the individual self and the Universal self implies harmonized spiritual relations and the absence of spiritual inequality that would otherwise keep them apart. Spiritual equality disapproves of any kind of barrier or privilege between man and man, or man and God. All beings are basically equal in the spiritual sense of being capable of attaining union with God. Therefore, equality between man and God is not only a physical but also a spiritual reality. All individuals are sparks of the divine and there is a divine element in each individual.

But mere belief in the spiritual equality of human beings is not sufficient by itself. For instance, all are equal in a democracy but there is no real sense of unity among them. The Western concept of equality lacks this sense of unity. This is brought about by the outlook of oneness of all, as the yoga of the *Bhagavad Gita* envisages. Its concept of spiritual equality or union with God visualizes treating others with love. The *Bhagavad Gita* (6.29) states: "The Yogi who is united in identity with the all-pervading, infinite consciousness, and looks on all with an equal eye, sees the Self as present in all beings, and all beings existing in the Self". Therefore, spiritual equality is incomplete without fraternal love. The spirit of brotherhood is an internal manifestation of love and spiritual equality of individuals is an external application of it. This makes the *Bhagavad Gita's* concept democratic and based on the spiritual equality, brotherhood and oneness of human beings.

The practice of the eight limbs of Patanjali Yoga, which the *Bhagavad Gita* also recommends, provides an ethical code of conduct, internal and external, for the individual. Internally, yoga requires cultivation of truth. A Yogi has to speak the truth, follow it and live in it. He proclaims it aloud to make the society an enlightened one. Externally, the practice of non-killing means to love all beings and become acclimatized to social life. The ethical ideals of non-violence, non-covetousness, non-stealing and steadfast commitment to truth, make the life of a Yogi a social one. Though the Yogic way of life is spiritually oriented, but according to the *Bhagavad Gita*, it also conveys a message of social unity.

A Yogi needs to be both a social being and a seeker after truth. He has to cultivate contacts with society. The *Bhagavad Gita's* stress on active life in society, implies that the individual not only need not shun society but must live in communion with it. A harmonized soul establishes harmonious relations with his fellow men and one who fails to do so cannot establish balanced relations with the divine being and maintain communion with it. As the *Bhagavad Gita* seeks to maintain balanced relations between man and God, and social and spiritual life, it also points out the necessity of moderation between physical and spiritual life.

The advocacy of a moderate physical life for the Yogi in the *Bhagavad Gita's* conception applies equally to the common man as to the ascetic and so is not a concession to human weakness. In fact, weakness of any kind is against its teachings. Its philosophy of moderation symbolizes strength only. Its outlook of physical moderation is evident when it says: "Yoga, which rids one of woe, is accomplished only by him who is regulated in diet and recreation, regulated in performing actions, regulated in sleeping and waking." (6.17).

In no uncertain terms, it condemns mortification of the flesh. It is of the view that neglect of the material needs of life emaciate the spirit of the individual. The moderation of the *Bhagavad Gita* points out the necessity of the physical life in combination with the spiritual life of the individual. While it is against any kind of indulgence, material or spiritual, it wants to stress the importance of both aspects of life, the ascetic and the normal, and harmonize them.

The application of the *Bhagavad Gita's* yogic imperative of moderation to society, means the maintenance of balanced reations between the individual and society on the basis of equality between the two. This would keep the individual and society within their proper limits for it takes into consideration the particular interests of the individual, on the one hand, and the general interests of the community, on the other. It does not subordinate the individual to society nor society to the individual. While the dominance of society would retard the growth of the individual, the pivotal place of the individual, whch ignores the interests of society, would hamper social growth and harmony. The concept of the *Bhagavad Gita* avoids the twin dangers of mastery and slavery. The individual behaves neither as a master of society nor as a slave to its authority. Society too, like the individual, is neither the master nor the servant of the individual.

In delineating interactions between man and man, the *Bhagavad Gita's* concept of human nature governs human relations. As man is essentially a spiritual being, he seeks to divinize his relations with his fellow men. He does not consider himself separate from others as they are his spiritual brothers. As the eternal spirit is inherent in all beings, he has to integrate with them. Human relations in society are to be based on the awakening of spiritual oneness of all individuals. In the absence of self-interest, there would be no ill-will, privileges and exploitation and so social relations would be suffused with selfless love, service and disinterested activity.

As the *Bhagavad Gita* maintains balanced relations between the internal and the external life of the individual, the individual and society, man and man, it also perfects the maintenance of the balance itself by the device of detached reason and disinterested activity. When the *Bhagavad Gita* (2.49) says that skill in action is yoga, it regards yoga as a perfect, harmonious blend of disinterested reason and activity. Mere cultivation of a detached frame of mind, as insisted upon by the yoga system of *Patanjali* is not the mark of spiritual perfection of the individual. To *act* in a detached frame of mind is what action in the world demands.

The yogic technique of social and political activity of the *Bhagavad Gita* depends upon the integration of ends and means. The means of activity are as important as the ends and it is the disinterested means that perfect and purify the reason of the individual. The *Bhagavad Gita* does not consider ends and means from the utilitarian point of view. It points out that dualities of pleasure and pain are transitory in nature and hold man in bondage. It considers activity not from the viewpoint of pleasure and pain but from the supreme consideration of individual freedom. According to its thinking, disinterested reason and activity culminate in freedom and liberation.

The Bhagavad Gita and Management Principles

The *Bhagavad Gita* records the dialogue between two men of action—Sri Krishna and Arjuna. So though it raises the discussion to a very high spiritual level it never loses sight of the prime objective—the need to act, to manage the battlefield of life.

In the *Bhagavad Gita*, Sri Krishna is a *sarathi*, the chariot driver. He does not bear weapons or fight but a great proportion of the warrior's success depends on the vision, skill and ability of the *sarathi*, who is his counselor, to manoeuvre him through the battlefield to take the best advantage of various opportunities. The warrior is the executive; the *sarathi* stands for top management. It is top management which plans, guides, directs and takes a holistic view before deciding where to operate and how. But when glory comes, the credit goes to the warrior, not to the *sarathi*. It is the non-appropriation of credit by top management that leads to success in management. As Lao Tze points out in another context, this is an eternal principle. "Those who do not claim credit always get that credit." This is often forgotten by senior managers.

To live within a social structure, to function effectively as part of a broader group, each individual is programmed according to the dictates and norms of social behaviour. We have already noted how the four classes have been made dependent by the *Bhagavad Gita* on skills and attitudes and not on birth. Arjuna is a Kshatriya. The Kshatriya is programmed to fight, to act, to manage, to attain noble ends, to punish evil-doers for crimes committed. All his strategies and tactical skills are aimed toward achieving these ends. But all that Arjuna can see around him are friends and relatives with whom he spent his childhood and grew up. Surely he was mistaken if he thought they were the enemy who needed to be destroyed and punished. After all, they are to him the known, and he cannot destroy the known as that would lead to disorder and chaos.

To cover his weakness he rationalizes. His efforts at justification and rationalization of his weaknesses make him look at other things than the problem in hand. He tries to foresee the effects of war and argues that future devastation of the social structure is reason enough for not taking up arms. He says:

> They behave as enemies, yet killing our own would be a sin for how could we be happy with a disturbed conscience? (1.37)
>
> Killing one's own results in a breakdown of established *dharma* (values). Once the social foundation of life crumbles, forces of anarchy take over. Chaos will result where order and peace prevailed. And as the cause of this chaos, we will have to live in eternal hell (1.39-43).

Management deals with people. Everyone is not brave. valiant, clever and sensitive. An individual may display characteristics of courage and cowardice, tolerance and intolerance, friendliness and enmity under different circumstances. However, no matter what the circumstance. the intellectual ability of man enables him to justify and rationalize his actions by constructing substantiative arguments in their favour. This is what Arjuna does. It is a classical example of mental bankruptcy often found in management when executives, instead of acting, spend their intellectual resources in constructing excuses for not doing anything. This is the situation in many organizations though today when massive changes are taking place in the environment, it is more necessary than ever before that management should have fast reflexes. foresight and determination. If executives are busy creating smoke screens or excuses for indecisiveness and non-performance, no organization can achieve its objectives.

Arjuna is demoralized, confused and refuses to take action. How to motivate him and make him perform efficiently is the problem facing Sri Krishna. Effective management is essentially an exercise in clarity of thought processes, and ability to piece together apparently dissonant elements into a harmonious whole and to implement plans flexibly while integrating them with the environment. For this managers need knowledge, aptitude and skills: knowledge of people, of the work to be performed and results to be achieved; the expertise to perform at least cost; and the skills needed to bring about high performance in action. The *Bhagavad Gita* is a lucid exposition on how Sri Krishna moves step by step towards creating performance orientation in the sadly dispirited Arjuna.

Often enough, it becomes an imperative of good management to be able to judge the magnitude of the crisis, locate the relevant issue needing to be resolved and take remedial measures. Defective or wrong analysis of the issue involved will lead to incorrect decisions. Consequently, many time one sees massive measures being taken to tackle simple problems, whereas the real harbingers of trouble are treated casually till one day the entire situation blows up in one's face. Identification of the gravity of issues is a key parameter of effective management and one of the skills needed for this is a sensitive approach to others. The teacher tests the situation to see if Arjuna's valour can be restored by a mild rebuke. Says Sri Krishna:

> From whence has this unmanly and shameful dejection come upon you, O Arjuna. Yield not to feebleness for it does not befit you. Cast off this petty faint-heartedness and wake up O Arjuna (2.2,3).

Arjuna's reply is a clear pointer to his mental agitation:

> My mind is in a turmoil with the thought of having to bear the sin of killing one's own. Help me, tell me what will be good for me. I take refuge in thee, for I know not. (2.7).

Arjuna's reply lays bare his heart. He acknowledges his inability to act in such a situation and seeks guidance. He has fought enemies before but here his emotions cloud his capacity to think clearly. He is lost. Never before has he tackled such foes and does not know what to do. He has two conflicting duties to perform: To punish the evil-doers facing him as the representative of the king and in furtherance of his duty as a Kshatriya; and to protect his family who also happen to be the evildoers. He does not know which *dharma* or duty to perform.

The teacher gauges the enormity of the problem facing his pupil and decides to tackle it first by explaining it in terms of values with which Arjuna is familiar. The arguments presented are substantiated by analogies to life and death, the physical and spiritual, the eternal and the ephemeral. Delving deeper, Sri Krishna goes on to the eternal Vedic verities which in Arjuna's world view were fundamental truths.

> You grieve for those who should not be grieved for; yet you speak words of wisdom. The wise grieve neither for the living nor for the dead (2.11).

> Remember, the Self is neither born nor does it die. It is omnipresent, whether in a body or otherwise. It is indestructible, invincible, never changing. Though the body may dissolve, the Self remains eternal (2.20).

The teacher relates Vedic values to the immediate context. Arjuna is exhorted to make use of the opportunity that has come his way and to dedicate himself to a proper performance of his social duty since duty to society overrides that due to his family. In any form of enterprise, shirking from one's duty and thereby missing an opportunity can only be construed as a cardinal sin. The answer is not in being inactive but in controlling the emotions and taking to that duty which is ethically and spiritually of a higher order.

Arjuna is listening but comprehension does not dawn on him. The teacher now begins to motivate him. He first appeals to his basic instinct of ego preservation. Arjuna is a warrior of repute. If he does not fight, he will be reduced to a laughing stock. What could be more denigrating to his reputation?[9]

As the appeals to Arjuna's egoistic instincts do not work Sri Krishna, ever flexible, moves on to a higher plane.

> Do not differentiate between pleasure and sorrow, gain or loss, victory or defeat. Then no sin can touch you for having fought your own.

> Keep your mind steadfast on God. Those who do not do so experience many feelings, many emotions and are led in many directions (2.38,41).

In life, desires lure us away from following the correct goals into chasing other objectives wherein we waste precious time. The only way not to be distracted is to examine all matters with a detached mind as only then can priorities be properly established. The person who works to the best of his ability, no matter how favourable or unfavourable the situation, is the truly liberated one. Such persons are veritably the very core and foundation of any successful enterprise — not racing after momentary short-term gains, nor wallowing in self-pity and misery under adverse conditions. They form the stable base which gives strength to the organization. For them the fundamental value is:

> The right to work is yours but not to expect desired results. However this is not an advice to stop working. Work one must but not with a particular selfish end in view (2.47).

There are many different perspectives on management; some extol profit making, some achievement and some others evaluation of performance in terms of a social cost-benefit matrix. One should not be swayed by any one view nor swing undecidedly from one to the other. The plethora of management texts, theories and gurus may create confusion of mind and lead to improper or incorrect action. Application of the fundamental core values brings peace of mind, clarity of vision and an ability to progress rapidly towards the goal. So work has not only to be performed with detachment but also with one-pointed concentration (2.41), knowledge (2.49), skill (2.50) and self-realization (2.51). Says Sri Krishna to Arjuna:

> When your mind which is bewildered and confused by conflicting opinions becomes poised and is in a state of equilibrium, then only will you get into yoga (2.53).

Steadfastness of goals, undistracted by transient attractions and the ability to be rational and calm are the qualities of successful managers. Those who get distracted by transient goals of personal enhancement at organizational cost or organizational enhancement at social cost cannot last beyond short periods of time. That manager is successful whose senses are under control, who is focussed towards the fundamental purpose of the enterprise and proceeds towards it unwaveringly through good times and bad.

In human behaviour, more specifically in the organizational context, three attributes assume critical significance: knowledge, skills and attitudes. With the strides that information technology has made today, knowledge is readily available to most. The means to gain skills are also not difficult to acquire. But what about attitudes? Today, in the last decade of the twentieth century, all over the world massive efforts are underway to upgrade the knowledge base and enhance the skills of managers. However, none of these efforts is capable of achieving success without the right attitudes.

As Sri Krishna tells Arjuna, the mind and senses can be controlled with effort but attitudes are more difficult to refashion. Our sense of discrimnation, our delight at certain things and dislike of others reinforce incorrect attitudes. To bring about attitudinal reorientation, one has to rise above dysfunctional patterns of behaviour dictated by sensory stimulation. The veil of distractions has to be lifted to get a glimpse of the liberating vision. Many ways and methods have been evolved throught the ages. But a superficial study of these methods will only lead the individual deeper into confusion and indecisiveness. Sometimes, unthinking acceptance of a particular view may have disastrous counsequences. Hence Sri Krishna counsels Arjuna to follow the path that comes naturally to him.

> One's own *dharma*, though imperfect, is better than the *dharma* of another well discharged. Better death in one's own *dharma*; the *dharma* of another is full of fear (3.35).

This applies not only to individuals but also to cultures and nations. For they too have their historically determined natures and codes of action. This is of obvious importance in a globalized system. Importing a successful model for transplantation in a different environment rarely succeeds. The good has to be analyzed in various models and permutated into a combination that is acceptable and workable in one's own distinctive environment.

The *Bhagavad Gita*, as we have seen, has modified the Vedic *Varnashrama* system by relating it to attitudes and not birth.

> I have created four classes to perform four kinds of functions, according to their qualities and abilities. Class is according to function, not function according to class. Though the creator, I am not attached to any of these classes (4.13).

In organizations this division of labour is seen again and again, varying in form and content with advances in technology but basically and structurally the same. Whatever be the organization, top management (the Brahmin) performs the function of conceptualization and the laying down of policy guidelines while the executives (the Kshatriyas) operationalize the policies through the formulation of plans and programmes. The financial health of the corporation is in charge of people (the Vaishyas) who are trained specifically for the purpose. Unspecialized jobs are performed by those who have neither the skill nor the training to execute any of the other functions (the Shudras).

An understanding of the nature of work and its functional divisions leads to liberation from conflict and confusion. The work of everyone is different but spiritually it leads to the highest result if performed well. It is not outer action that is important but the inner attitude—the drive towards the attainment of perfection. This comprehension helps to remove the misunderstandings that arise between the different classes in organizations, where one level feels that greater advantages accrue to others due to their relatively higher position in the hierarchy.

Today products have also to meet the criteria of high quality. Quality and the quest for perfection are inseparable. Perfection is inherent in the relationship between work and God. God is perfection, perfection of ideas, perfection of deeds, perfection of intentions. God is just as much in the perfection of the quality of our products, services and processes as in our powers of conceptualization. When we achieve perfection in any objective, we are filled with a sense of total bliss, which is heaven. We create our own heaven and our own hell through our actions. The way to God is through the best performance of work but without attachment to short-term results for self. This is the call of the hour, the so-called mystique of the East, which is applicable equally to management and religious philosophy. Says the *Bhagavad Gita*,

> Perform action fixed in yoga, be even-minded in success and failure, for yoga is perfection in action (2.48).

The *Bhagavad Gita* lays great stress on the attainment of knowledge. It says: Even if you be the most sinful of all sinners, yet you shall cross over all sin by the raft of knowledge alone (4.36).

In the concept of the *Bhagavad Gita*, knowledge is of two types. One that is derived from the experiences of others. This is *gyana*, knowledge that encapsules the lessons learnt through practice. The second kind of knowledge, *vigyana*, is the intuitive knowledge that comes out of the depths of the human being revealing itself to those who have striven dedicatedly without any selfish motive except to realize the supreme consciousness.

Vigyana is the capacity for abstract thinking. To develop this capacity, which is absolutely essential for good management, it is necessary to create an environment where concentration and reflection are encouraged. The seat, both in the material and spiritual sense, from which thought is to originate, must be such as to be optimally conducive for it. Too high or too low a seat (high and low being considered in the psychological sense) may bring with it thought processes that would deflect one from focussing on the supreme goal. One has to steadfastly overcome the mental barriers of emotions like pride, ago and hurt to be able to reflect on the past logically and scientifically.[10]

Integrating the intuitive mind with the rational in thought and deed is a precondition to developing an ability to take a macroview of situations and take the appropriately correct managerial decisions. Too close an involvement precludes this. An old Chinese proverb says that to see a forest, you have to step back from the trees. Balance, objectivity and logical thought, prepare the ground for clear level-headed thinking and decision-making. But that is not all. What is even more crucial is steadfastness in attaining the laid down objectives. Says the *Bhagavad Gita*, "The Yogi is one whose mind is unwaveringly steady like a lamp in a windless place" (6.19).

Different kinds of work and ways of working reflect varied value systems, from the ideal to the commonly practised to the undesirable. It is not that these methods have to be rigid, that one who is following a lesser path cannot make a mid-course correction. Flexibility is at the core of sound management; flexibility that aids the individual to overcome shortcomings, to improve and better the style of functioning that helps achieve the ultimate goal of liberation.

The *Bhagavad Gita*'s system of management is flexible in the extreme. It is not bound to any particular form of structure for it stresses processes and values. Its concept of sacrifice makes the system dynamic and its insistence on a non-hierarchical order (since every one has to follow his own *dharma* and not the *dharma* of another[11]) leads to a networking of individuals which attains optimality by constantly adjusting to each other as well as the fast changing environment.

Another area stressed by the *Bhagavad Gita* is the attaining of happiness and bliss through yoga (6.28). Ever since the first man trod the surface of the earth, mankind has ceaselessly striven for happiness. He sought it first in food that assuaged the pangs of hunger and for a short while, that was happiness. But it was not enough for the cold winds raked his skin, the rains lashed him while the summer sun scorched his body. When he found shelter from the elements and other lurking dangers in the environment, that too was happiness. Only it did not last. For he wanted company; he wanted the security of a social system where he could both give and receive love and affection; he wanted others to recognize him, praise him, elevate him to a high status and come to him for help and advice. All these brought happiness but again it did not last. For a while, he was content but then restlessness stirred inside him and he sought happiness anew. Some sought it one way, some in another, depending on their motives and methods of seeking. The *Bhagavad Gita* goes beyond the pure surface happiness, which is not long-lasting, and suggests the following of self-control, serenity and poise (6.6,7) as the way to yogic bliss (6.27).

Conclusion

The *Bhagavad Gita* makes the eternal Vedic principles contextual to the time it was enunciated and does this by integrating the different forms of yoga. The yoga of the *Bhagavad Gita* is a philosophical system that treats all life as a management enterprise. A successful manager needs knowledge of all factors that he has to manage and all that is beyond but which directly or indirectly impinge on his micro-environment. One who has acquired a realistic vision of the totality finds himself rising over narrow, short-term, individualistic motives that generally drive human beings. The larger vision encompasses the good of mankind and the welfare of society. The way that everything is integrated into the One (and not just "the One spoken of differently" as in the Rig Veda) is shown to Arjuna as the *Vishwaroopa*. On seeing this vision of the integrated One, Arjuna exclaims: I see in you everything, the Creator, the Destroyer, all grades of being, having infinite forms on all sides...(11.15-18).

According to the *Bhagavad Gita* everything has to be integrated. The managerial principle flowing from this is to be impartial, not to favour any one goal, any one mode, any one or group of persons. The goal being total integration within the environmental constraints, the manager has to select the appropriate strategy for achieving this integrated good. He is not to be swayed by happiness or sorrow, ego or nepotism, greed or desire. His impartiality ensures the success of his mission and he is the true *sthitapragya* — the one who is steadfast in enlightenment (2.55-72).

This impartiality arises from having drunk deep of the eternally moving stream of knowledge, of being no longer swayed by the external temptations of tangible, material success for he knows how insignificant these are in the context of eternal bliss. One also becomes aware that entanglement in these desires is accompanied by misery when they are not fulfilled. But knowledge is not enough, it is only the guiding beacon. To be liberated, one has to overcome desire for wealth, happiness, recognition and anger at non-achievement of these. Those who can do this, according to the *Bhagavad Gita* (5.29) rise to the plane of eternal truth that brings not only happiness and contentment but also peace. Such managers radiate joyous bliss and their decisions bring happiness, sooner or later, to the world in general.

The ideal enunciated by the *Bhagavad Gita* is that a good manager has to not only manage but also to lead, to think ahead, to evaluate with an open mind and take decisions that begin to concertize today's vision for tomorrow. Viewing an issue from many different angles is necessary to develop a holistic perspective. Such knowledge comes through work tempered with contemplation and genuine altruism. It is the merger of the two that creates a great manager and is at the heart of sound management.

Management is often considered to be the prerogative of human beings, that too an advanced group of humans who by virtue of certain qualitative and quantitative abilities are in a position to organize and manage. However, a look at the wonders that exist in the world around us reveals this as a short-sighted view. Nature is the greatest manager of all for she endows her creations with the ability to react and adapt to situations thus ensuring survival over long stretches of time. The highly systematized life in an anthill or a beehive is a case in point. Through their own methods of communication, ants and bees exhibit division of labour, delegation and a very highly evolved system of coordination. Shoals of fish or migration of birds are a study in the formulation and observance of the rules of group behaviour. Thus, management practice, stemming from little understood processes of thinking, is common to all forms of life and not just human beings who occupy a microcosm of time and space in the history of the universe. This is pointed out in the *Bhagavad Gita* (10.24-31) where it says that the Lord is also the ocean, mountains, trees, horses, elephants, cows, etc. Human beings should not look down on nature but learn from her.

What sets humans apart from the other beings, however, is the power to conceptualize thought and express it in logical constructs, using linguistic symbols. Whereas the other forms of life work though the senses, humans are capable of both sensual perception and thinking which is rational, intuitive or a blend of the two. Sensual thinking is reactive while rational and intuitive thinking brings about pro-active behaviour. Using visual methods, imagery and verbal-logical techniques, such thinking leads to a conceptualization of processes, tasks and objectives, of their complexities and conditionalities. This is the predecessor of operational thinking; the application to situations of a series of optional sequences for achieving the same goal. And the uniqueness of the human mind lies in creating a storehouse of knowledge that future generations can use to refine and purify their thinking processes to manage the changing environment more effectively.

Knowledge then is the result and cause of thinking, for knowledge stirs the human intellect and the curiosity factor simulates further thought. This intellectual exercise results in the addition and enrichment of existing knowledge, in the process overturning or negating some established theories and principles, at other times reinforcing them. As the dimensions of an individual's knowledge increase, so does his ability to take a more complete view of an issue. Unidirectional knowledge focusses one's thinking in a single dimension which may not coincide with that of others involved in the same task. And this gives rise to conflict: conflict in the perceptions of goals, conflict in motivations, conflict in attitudes and conflict in the process of problem resolution. A multifaceted outlook, coupled with rationality in selection of solutions and keeping the thought processes in tune with the environmental requisites is what may be called the appropriate use of knowledge.

The last verse of the *Bhagavad Gita* brings all the management principles to a conclusion. Says Sanjaya, the minister of the king Dhritrashta after he has heard the whole discourse between Sri Krishna and Arjuna: "Wherever there is Krishna, the master of yoga, and Arjuna, the wielder of the bow, there (in that society) shall be found wealth, victory, general welfare, and unwavering justice and ethical sense — this is my conviction".

The verse refers to the confluence, in each person, of two energies needed to achieve total human welfare: The first is the energy of yoga, the energy of vision, of calm spirituality, represented by Sri Krishna, who, in the Mahabharata war did not take part in the actual fighting, but only gave sagely guidance to Arjuna; and the second is the energy of intense and efficient action, represented by Arjuna, the hero of action. This represents the combination of contemplation and action, vision and implementation, which the *Bhagavad Gita* and the Chinese philosophy of Taoism call the state of being sagely within and kingly without. When this is achieved all management and administration achieves the highest level of efficiency.

The first fruit of that confluence, says the verse, is *shri*, economic prosperity, which needs, not only knowledge and hard work, but also the capacity for dedication and teamwork, which is the gift of character, dedication and detachment.

The second fruit of that confluence is *vijaya*, victory, which means, success accompanying every project, every endeavour. The failures or the low-level performances of many projects ad undertakings can be traced to the absence of that confluence. Wherever success has been registered, we can detect the presence of that confluence of calmness and activity, of yoga and intense action.

The third fruit of that confluence is *bhutih*, general welfare. *Shri* and *bhutih* together constitute welfare, which is a socio-economic and cultural objective. According to the *Bhagavad Gita* to achieve that objective, we need a fourth value.

And the verse refers to that fourth value as *dhruva nitih*, constant justice and ethical sense. No political system, no economics, no society, no managerial enterprise can be healthy without unwavering justice and ethical sense. This is the value called *dharma*,which holds the scale even between individuals and individuals, between groups and groups; by favouring one individual or group and discriminating against another individual or group we increase injustice in society and increase social choas. The management system of the *Bhagavad Gita* is thus more an art than a science, depends on inner calmness accompanying outward action, of having peace and happiness of all as the end to be achieved through a feeling of justice towards all as the manner of getting harmony whether in society, polity or an organization. The process of yoga is the integration of all the inner and outer activities of humanity — in the individual, society, the cosmos.

REFERENCES

1. All citations, unless stated otherwise, are from the *Bhagavad Gita*.
2. Sri Aurobindo, *Essays on the Gita* (Pondicherry: Aurobindo Ashram, 8th ed., 1987), p. 117.
3. *Swadharma* means the law of being, the rule or law of action of the individual something that grows out of his own nature or his *swabhava*.

4. Christopher Isherwood, *Vedanta for the Western World* (London: Allen and Unwin, 1951), p. 3.
5. Swami Ranganathananda, *Eternal Values for a Changing Society* (Bombay: Bharatiya Vidya Bhawan, 1971), p. 479.
6. Cf. *Bhagavad Gita*, 3.35 which states,

   "Better one's own duty, though seemingly imperfect, than to perform that of someone else; for that is the way to destruction."
7. George Feuerstein, *The Yogasutra of Patanjali: A new translation* (Folkstone: Davidson and Sons, 1979).
8. Anirvan, *Buddhiyoga of the Gita and Other Essays*, quoted in "Buddhiyoga in the Bhagavadgita" in *Hindu Spirituality*, ed. K. Sivaraman (Delhi: Motilal Banarsidas, 1995), p. 205.
9. *Bhagavad Gita*, 2.24.
10. Cf. *Bhagavad Gita*, 6.11, 12.
11. *Bhagavad Gita*, 18.47.

7

GANDHIAN MANAGEMENT

The Vedic management system as elaborated in the Vedas and the Upanishad is a normative system while the *dharmashastras* actualize the same system in the context of the conditions prevalent in those times. The normative system enunciated by the Vedas and Upanishads is, as we have seen, a decentarlized system integrated by *rita* and *dharma*.

The normative Vedic management system as its fundamental foundations had the following elements:

- the management system was suffused with Vedic values and tried to integrate the worlds of spirit and matter through sacrifice and *rita*,
- the system laid more stress on process (yoga and *dharma*) than structure,
- the system was non-hierarchical and depended on trusting the individual rather than on a centralized command and control system; and
- accountability of top management was through the principle of stewardship.

But management is not only theory but also praxis. In this context, it is not adequate to have a normative theory of Vedic management, or a system which worked in the time of *dharmashastras*, but also to see whether it is capable of being practised in today's world.

One person who did this is Gandhi in the earlier part

of the twentieth century when he set up an organization in his struggle to free India from British rule. His success against one of the most powerful Empires known to history merits study in understanding the concepts, objectives and principles on which he organized the movement against British rule.

The historicity of British rule in India was Gandhi's starting point and a constant frame of reference. He was deeply puzzled and troubled by it. He wondered why the British who had come to India in the first place, had been able to consolidate their rule and make it acceptable to their subjects, what it had done to Indians and how Indians should respond to it. His reflections led him to conclude that the answers were to be found in the character of modern civilization. The British had come to India because of the inner compulsions of the modern economy; they had been able to consolidate their rule because of their ability to legitimize it in the ideological language of modern civilization; their rule, thus, was not merely political but also moral and cultural in nature; and so the response to it had also to be political, moral and cultural.

In Gandhi's view the British came to India in search of new markets for their goods. They needed to trade because their economic life was geared to mass production that could not suvive without turning the whole world into a vast market. As to why their economics was so geared, he gave two different answers. Sometimes he pointed to its capitalist character and attributed over-production to its search for profits. More often he argued that capitalism was itself a product of the 'materialist' view of life. It was because humanity was defined as a creature of infinite desires that the constant satisfaction of its apparently endless wants and the accumulation of wealth acquired moral legitimacy in capitalism. Gandhi was convinced that imperialism in one form or another was inherent in modern civilization though he was unclear as to when and why the materialist view emerged and why it was able to replace the older 'spiritual' view with such ease.

As to why the British had been able to consolidate their rule, Gandhi's answer was more complex. He rejected the widely held view that they had a superior army, as also the views that the innocent and absent-minded Indians, ill-tutored in the ways of the world, had been outwitted by the wily foreigners. In Gandhi's view the explanation was two-fold. First, the Indians had long been in the habit of fighting among themselves and some of them turned to the newly arrived East India Company for financial and military help. The Company began to play an increasingly important role in Indian political life and its interference came to be accepted as legitimate and necessary.[1] Over time it played off one group against another and thereby broadened and consolidated its rule. 'The English have not taken India; we have given it to them', Gandhi argued. 'To blame them...is to perpetuate their rule'.[2] It is interesting to note how Gandhi internalized the problem in the manner of the Upanishads and blamed the Indians rather than the British for the establishment and perpetuation of British rule.

Gandhi's second explanation went deeper and centred on the ideological role of the concept of civilization. The British were able to consolidate their rule because the Indians had become enamoured of their civilization. By British civilization Gandhi meant both its industrial products and moral and political values, practices and institutions. In his view the two were inseparable and to desire industrial products was to accept and want the constitutive values and institutions of British civilization. Since the Indians had become enamoured of British civilization, they traded in its products, thereby making it profitable and worthwhile for the British to rule over India. Since the Indians had also been bewitched (the Sanskrit word used by Gandhi was *moha*) by British moral and political values, they did not find British rule morally insulting and outrageous, and on the contrary thought it highly desirable and in their long-term interest.

The Indians, of course, had their own civilization and distinct views on what constituted a civilized man and society. These had to be discredited and their self-confidence undermined if British civilization was to strike roots. Accordingly the British embarked upon a programme of systematic 'scientific indoctrination' devised and enforced by intellectuals all too ready to place their knowledge at the service of the Empire. British historians argued that pre-British India was a disorderly and chaotic society that had never known peace and stability and that British rule alone stood as a shield against chaos. British anthropologists produced biased accounts of Indian customs and practices and contended that they were all primitive and needed to be changed. Gandhi observed, 'The English...have a habit of writing history; they pretend to know the customs and practices of every society...They beat their own drums, and hypontise us into believing them. In our gullibility we believe all that'.[3]

For Gandhi, British imperialism dominated India at three related but different levels. At the political level the arrogant colonial government oppressed the Indian people and denied them the right to run their affairs themselves. At the economic level it exploited and impoverised them, destroyed their indigenous industries and subordinated their interests to those of British industry. In Gandhi's view this was far more disturbing than political oppression. At the most disturbing moral and cultural level, British imperialism destroyed the identity and integrity of Indian civilization and turned the Indians into 'brown' Englishmen.

To Gandhi, British imperialism was unacceptable not only because of its political and economic consequence, but its moral and cultural impact. The struggle against it had therefore to be mounted and independence obtained at all three levels, especially the moral and cultural.

Gandhi's critique of British rule thus encompassed political, economic, cultural and moral aspects. He was acutely aware of its economic motivation and highlighted the grave economic damage it had done and was doing to the country. He used the language of national honour, pride and dignity to rouse the people. He argued that political independence was important not only as an expression of India's pride and a necessary means to stop its economic exploitation but also to preserve its civilization, without which political independence would remain fragile. The economic explotation had to be ended not only to sustain Indian independence and improve the living conditions of its people but also to preserve the social and economic basis of its civilization.

Gandhian Critique of Modern Civilization

To Gandhi the conflict was not between the Indian and European or between the Eastern and Western civilizations, but was really between the ancient and modern. As he put it, there is 'no such thing as Western or European civilization, but there is modern civilization'.[4] According to Parikh, this apparently trivial redefinition was in fact intended to alter the terms of the debate in his favour and achieve several ideological and political advantages. First, he was able to reject the then prevalent view that the East and the West were radically different and shared nothing in common. For Gandhi such a doctrine had no basis in fact, denied the fundamental unity of mankind enunciated by the Vedas and bred cultural parcochialism. Second, he was able to attack modern civilization without attacking the West. He greatly admired Christanity, such modern writers as Tolstoy, Ruskin and Thoreau and several Western values and practices, and wished to exclude them from his criticism. Third, the distinction enabled Gandhi to argue that modern civilization was of relatively recent origin in the West and that its pre-modern counterpart was very different and more like the Indian. He hoped thereby to remind the West of its earlier traditions and values, evoke its temporarily suppressed historical memories and elicit its support for his fight against modern civilization. Fourth, by arguing that industrial civilization was modern and 'still very young', Gandhi intended to suggest that it lacked the wisdom and maturity conferred by a long history, an important argument in a country like India that revered age. Finally, Gandhi hoped to convice his contrymen that in fighting modern civilization they were not being reactionary. They were only combating the arrogance and impetuosity of a historical upstart and helping to preserve the permanent values of the whole of mankind, including the West. The idea of saving the soul of their misguided masters tickled Indian pride and made Gandhi's message more acceptable even to the Westernized elites.[5]

In Gandhi's view, modern civilization was grounded in a fatally flawed theory of man. Unlike Vedic civilization which was soul-or spirit-centred, the modern was body-centred and in that sense 'materialistic'. For the body was the seat of the senses, and thus of wants and desires. By their very nature desires recurred with regularity, were never satiated, and were interrelated with one desire always giving rise to others.

A body-centred or materialist view attributed two basic properties to man, namely selfishness and an inifinite multiplicity of wants which it regarded as natural and legitimate. A civilization based on such a flawed view necessarily lacked moral and spiritual depth, had no guiding principles to decide what desires deserved to be satisfied and within what limits, thus distorting the human psyche and suffusing it with the spirit of violence.

Modern civilization was therefore, to Gandhi, propelled by greed and want. It was controlled by 'a few capitalist owners' who had only one aim, to make profit, and only one means to do so, to produce goods that satisfied people's desires and wants. They had a vested interest in constantly whetting jaded appeties, creating new wants and a moral climate in which not to want goods and to keep pace with the latest fashions was to be abnormal and archaic. Indeed, since restriction of desires, the very emblem of human dignity, threatened to cause mass unemployment, throw the economic system out of gear and cause human suffering, self-disciplie was seen as anti-social and immoral. No surprisingly men saw themselves not as self-determining moral subjects but as consumers or objects for the satisfication of externally-induced wants.

As a result, in the Gandhian concept, people's moral life suffered a profound distortion. First, it become as abstract as the men it was supposed to relate to, and was reduced to a set of externally legislated and enforced impersonal rules. Second, morality was seen as a painful restriction of freedom of choice. Third, the society being one of basically amoral and unrelated beings was characterized by a climate of suspicion, fear, hostility and tension. Fourth, in the absence of goodwill and mutual concern modern life lacked roots and vitality. Man took care not to harm others lest they should in turn harm him thus reducing morality to reciprocal egoism or enlightened self-interest and sustaining it by fear.

The result was that modern man spent most of his energy trying to stablize himself in a hostile and unsteady environment. He had neither the inclination nor the ability to slow down the tempo of his life, relax, compose himself reflect on his pattern of life and nurture the inner springs of energy. He lived outside himself and exhausted himself physically and spiritually.[6]

In Gandhi's view, the exploitation of one's fellow men was built into the very structure of modern civilization. Consumers were constantly manipulated into desiring things they did not need and which were not in their long-term interest. Workers were made to do boring jobs at subsistence wages, the poor were treated with contempt and held responsible for their own misfortunes, the weaker nations were conquered, mercilessly oppressed and used as dumping grounds for surplus goods and as sources of cheap raw material and labour.

It was therefore hardly surprising that such a civilization needed to be sustained by massive violence. In a society of ambitious, competitive and mutually fearful men, one could not survive without developing a psyche involving violence against other men at both the personal and collective levels. Since everyone felt threatened by others he had to rely on the use of threat of moral and physical violence ultimately backed by the concentrated violence of the modern state.

Gandhi argued that the highly centralized and bureaucratic modern state enjoying and zealously guarding its monopoly of political power was a necessary product of modern civilization. Competitive and aggressive men ruthlessly pursuing selfish interests needed to be held together by a well-armed State. Since they lacked the bonds of goodwill and mutual concern, their relations could only be regulated by impersonal rules imposed and enforced by a powerful State. Besides the centralization of production in the modern economy created social and economic problems of national and international magnitude, and required a centralized political agency to deal with the unemployment, poverty and the social and economic inequalities created by the modern economy. Moreover, the centralized modern State was also necessary to protect international markets and overseas investments.

Although convinced that the foundation of modern civilization was 'rotten', Gandhi did not dismiss it altogether and praised what he took to be its three great achievements. First, he admired its scientific spirit of inquiry. He observed:

> ...I have discovered that underlying the fever that fills the soul of the West, there is a restless search for Truth. I value that spirit. Let us study...(ourselves)...in that spirit of scientific inquiry.[7]

For Gandhi the scientific spirit meant rational inquiry, the search for the Truth in place of being satisfied with tradition, and implied intellectual curiosity and critical examination of established systems.

The second great achievement of modern civilization, in Gandhi's view, was in understanding the natural world. Being body-centred it concentrated on improving the material conditions of life by developing the ability to anticipate and control natural calamities, eliminate diseases, improve health and public hygiene, prolong life and reduce or relieve human drudgery. It also developed transport and communications, brought the world closer and improved the material quality of life.

Third, Gandhi considered modern civilization to have greatly contributed to the social side of life. It had cultivated civic virtues, respect for rules, the capacity to subordinate the personal to the collective interest, public morality, mutual respect and punctuality.

Modern civilization was thus a highly complex human achievement, and the response to it had to be equally complex. Its foundation was shaky but it had genuine achievements that could not easily be combined with those of Indian civilization. Since they were secured within a fundamentally different famework, Gandhi was of the view that they had to be purged of their distortions and 'purified' before they could be incorporated into the Indian system.[8]

Gandhi's Conceptual Framework

In his fight against British imperialism Gandhi thought it necessary to have both a conceptual framework and an organization that could challenge the well-entrenched British administration. Both of these were necessarily to be founded on the values inherent in Indian civilization in view of his critique of the modern variant. He turned to Indian thought and values to establish his conceptual framework before going on to reorganize the Congress party. His conceptual framework had to be based on Indian cultural values and also had to have an economic content.

To Gandhi the most important cultural value that needed to be incorporated was that of non-violence. Gandhi, who was influenced by the cultures of India and England, the religions of Hinduism, Jainism, Buddhism, Islam and Christianity, and the writings of John Ruskin, Leo Tolstoy and Henry David Thoreau, put the peculiar stamp of his genius upon the theory of non-violence which he had originally drawn from Patanjali's *Yogasutra*. He confronted the problems of British imperialism, modern industrialism, racism, classism, etc., in his own unique way and flowing from his concept of non-violence.

The second postulate that activated him was the search for truth. The method of inquiry and mode of action that Gandhi used in his search for truth is what he called *satyagraha*. *Satya* means truth and *graha* means adherence to truth. Satyagraha thus to him meant adherence to truth.

Gandhi's life was an experiment with truth (*satya*) and the means to achieve the truth was throoough *ahimsa* (non-violence). The full force of *ahimsa*, explicitly stated, meant "action based on the refusal to do harm".[9] For Gandhi, *ahimsa* (non-violence, or love, as he called it) was the means, and *satya* (truth) was the end, and the debate on the means-end continuum was meaningless, for they were irrevocably tied to one another by the doctrine of *karma*. "The means may be likened to a seed, the end to a tree, and there is just the same inviolable connection between the means and the end as there is between the seed and the tree... We reap exactly what we sow".[10]

Not to hurt any living thing was only a part of *ahimsa*, that was its least expression. "The principle of *ahimsa* is hurt by every evil thought, by undue haste, by lying, by wishing ill to anybody".[11] According to Gandhi's interpretation of *ahimsa*, "it is not merely a negative state of harmlessness but it is a positive state of love, of doing good even to the evil-doer. However, neither does it means tolerating injustice. On the contrary, *ahimsa* requires not only resistance but also conversion of the wrongdoer".[12]

If there is a dogma in Gandhian thought, says Bondurant, "it centres here, that the only test of truth is action based on refusal to do harm".[13] This is one principle of *ahimsa* that Gandhi adhered to until the end. To him the supreme and the only means to the discovery of social truths was through *ahimsa*.

Because we covet things and seek pleasure, we are in a constant state of competition, obsessively seeking self-gratification at the cost of others, plus putting ourselves in a state of violence. Hence, the fulfilment of *ahimsa* is difficult, if not impossible, without self-sacrifice and selfessness. For Gandhi, *ahimsa* means universal love; and in its dynamic form it means conscious suffering. It does not mean meek surrender to unjust acts or laws, but confronting the oppressor with a firm conviction and single-minded honest purpose.

Gandhi kept the *Bhagavad Gita s* dictum in mind:

By reason of delusion man takes wrong to be right.

Effort is within man's control, not the fruit thereof. All he has to do, therefore, is to decide his course of conduct or duty on each occasion and preserve it unconcerned about the result. Fulfilment of one's duty in the spirit of detachment and selflessness leads to freedom.[14]

Gandhi was profoundly influenced by the *Bhagavad Gita*, which shaped his perspective, in general and his economic views, in particular. In the eyes of Gandhi the *Bhagavad Gita* was a complete and reasoned moral code which satisfied the heart as well as the intellect. He got from the *Bhagavad Gita* the realization that life is given to us for service and not for enjoyment. Man has to, by virtue of being a human being, perform an innate duty to serve Truth by serving his fellowmen and the life process in general. Such action is to be performed as service for the sake of service. It involves self-sacrifice or *yagya* for the welfare of others. By so rising above self-interest human beings fulfil their destiny and become integrated with the true self within.

The aspect of self-sacrifice, as advocated by Gandhi, according to Bondurant, may be the least acceptable to the Western mind. "Yet, such sacrifice may well provide the ultimate means of realizing that characteristic so eminent in Western moral philosophy: the dignity of the individual".[15] For Gandhi flowing from his concept of self-sacrifice, society was not possible without individual freedom and dignity. "No society can possibly be built on a denial of individual freedom".[16]

In making a distinction between man and the system, Gandhi highlighted the primacy of the individual. The system, whether it be social, political, economic, or religious, should be geared toward the betterment of the individual. When a system becomes harmful to the well-being of man, it must be mended or ended, altered or abolished.[17]

The *Bhagavad Gita's* concept of self-sacrifice and service as the method of integrating society and as the way to the welfare of all through *lokasangraha* made

Gandhi a firm believer in *sarvodaya*—man's duty to serve all living beings in the universe.[18] But a selfish, self-centred person would be seeking only self-gratification. Hence, "the path of service can hardly be trodden by one who is not prepared to renounce self-interest...The duty of renunciation differentiates mankind from the beast".[19] Renunciation here does not mean abandoning that world, for the would be cowardice. In line with the teaching of the *Bhagavad Gita*, it means detachment from worldly posessions and desires, so that one can immerse himself or herself in selfless activity for the welfare of all.

Gandhian principles recognize that the individual is primary and the rest of the social institutions are secondary and are there to serve him. Man, the operator of the system, needs all the help available. Thus, we can have a legitimate quarrel with the system that is evil, but we should have no quarrel or hatred for the people in whose name and by whom the system is operated. Gandhi championed the cause of the underprivileged, and the cause of those to whom palpable injustice may have been done, to purify and regenerate society. "While working for the mending or ending or certain outmoded institutional patterns, Gandhi placed his main reliance upon sensitized consciences, upon regenerated human beings for abiding change in society".[20] His prayer for another was "...not, God give him the light that Thou has given me, but give him all the light and truth he needs for the highest development."[21]

To Gandhi it was evident that only in this way could radical socio-political change be brought about in a non-violent manner and on the basis of truth. And socio-political change was to him the necessary precondition for strengthening Indian society and ousting British rule from India.

Gandhian Socio-economics

Gandhi used the above principles in developing an economic system based on ancient Indian thought. Conventional economic emphasises self interest by building upon the notion of utilitarianism. Gandhi, however, rejected

Bentham's concept of the greatest good of the greatest number in favour of the greatest-good-of-all or *sarvodaya*. According to him:

> I do not believe in the doctrine of the greatest good for the greatest number. It means in its nakedness that in order to achieve the supposed good of fifty-one per cent, the interest of forty-nine per cent may be, or rather should be sacrificed.[22]
>
> The utilitarian's (sphere of destruction) has no limit. Judged by the standard of non-violence the late war was wholly wrong. Judged by the utilitarian standard, each party has justified it according to its idea of utility...Precisely on the same ground the anarchist justifies his assassinations. But none of these acts can possibly be justified on the greatest-good-of-all-principle.[23]

Gandhi's thought led him to postulate a grand design of an ideal social order: A non-violent, non-exploitative, humanistic and egalitarian society. This social order embodied the fundamental philosophy of his life. He approached all facets of society—its economics, its politics and sociology—from the philosophical premises—truth and non-violence—that governed his entire life. For him, therefore, economics could not be 'ethically neutral'. In his own words: "That economics is untrue which disregards moral values. This extension of the law of non-violence in the domain of economics means nothing less than the introduction of moral values...".[24] With the appearance of morality in Gandhian economics, we also witness the demise of the 'eeconomic man', the core paramenter of mainstream economics.

Gandhi was not an economist in the ordinary sense of the term. In his own way, however, he constructed a model which he claimed to be practical and operational in a given environment. He sketched out, in considerable details, its basic goal(s), its structure, its components, its modus operandi, its data and its variables. Viewed as an economic system, it has its own management scheme and its own techno-structure. It is not a static but a dynamic model, embodying a Gandhian theory of growth. He wrote: "The end to be sought is human happiness combined with full mental and moral growth. I use the adjective moral as synonymous with spiritual".[25]

He did not overlook the purely material goals in his economic system. Any viable economic system, he insisted, must have the production capability to meet social demand for the basic necessities of life—food, clothing, shelter, and other essential prerequisites for survival. But he rejected the pursuit of economic abundance for its own sake. He considered such abundance, dictated by the multiplicity of seemingly insatiable human wants, as demoralizing. He was unconvinced that economic abundance, measured by the physical volume of goods and services, is either a necessary or a sufficient condition for individual or social welfare. On the contrary, an incessant drive for economic abundance, through accumulation, competition, and technological innovation, he felt, would promote economic aggression, exploitation, and violence in society.[26]

The production goal of a Gandhian economic system has been stated by Huq as "the maximization of socially necessary goods and services, and the minimization of luxuries and superfluous goods, constrained not only by the availability of scarce resources but also by an overriding moral purpose".[27] The production and consumption of luxuries to stimulate effective demand was repugnant to Gandhian economic philosophy. He was opposed to such 'conspicious consumption' on both moral and economic grounds.

Another parameter of Gandhi's model was localized production or *swadeshi*. Modern economics stresses individualistic mobility and competition on the basis of self-interest. Gandhi's doctrine of non-self-interest, on the other hand, emphasises the social virtues of loyalty and cooperation. No other Gandhian concept illustrates this better than that of *swadeshi*, the spirit in us which restricts us to the use and service of our immediate surroundings to the exclusion of the more remote.

Swadeshi can be seen as the application of the principles of the *Bhagavad Gita* to one's immediate environment. In the sphere of economics, it would give a priority or preference for locally grown and manufactured goods. The doctrine of *swadeshi* could also be applied to the labour market: Employers are to exhaust first whatever pool of local and unemployed workers there is before hiring more suitable labour from other towns or regions. Similarly, the workers would be more reluctant to leave a local employer in spite of more attractive job offers elsewhere. In short, economic agents living together in a community, region, or country, should first and foremost explore all possibilities to do business with each other before going outside in order to get a better deal. *Swadeshi* demands the sacrifice of utility for the sake of loyalty. The alleged gains of violating *swadeshi* (lower commodity price, higher quality, etc.) would tend to be more than counteracted by almost zero transport costs and the (non-market) costs of community decay. At the same time, Gandhi warned that *swadeshi* should not be made a fetish. Efficiency was also to be maintained. According to him:

> (One) should use only things that are produced by (one's) immediate neighbours and serve those industries by making them efficient and complete where they might be wanting.[28]

The Foundations of the Gandhian System

We have already stated that Gandhi's is a humanistic and holistic concept encompassing politics, sociology, psychology, ethics, economics and ecology and based on his philosophical outlook. The four parameters of his social philosophy are:

- Truth exists in and beyond man in an absolute, eternal and living essence.
- The purpose of all life and evolution is to realize truth. For humankind this translates into the need for self-realization, to know one's self.
- While truth is the end, nonviolence is the means. Truth and non-violence are ultimately two sides of

the same coin. One implies the other. Self-realization knows no distintion between ends and means. From this follows the all important principle that we cannot realize truth without giving up the means/ ends dichotomy.

- Human truth is always relative. Although we have the innate need to perfect ourselves, no man is perfect.
- Truth as we can apprehend it is always personal, subjective, and, to that extent, relative to our individual context of culture, history and psychology. In this Gandhi followed the Rig Veda which states.

"The wise speak of what is One in many ways".[29]

From these four philosophical paramenters emphasizing non-violence as the key to realization of truth, and stressing the relativity of human perception due to subjectivity and cultural differences, we arrive at the following foundational premises pertaining to Gandhi's thought:

- Economics, ethics, politics and religion constitute an indivisible whole. As such, Gandhi had no kind words about conventional economics which led to a acquisitive and therefore a violent society. According to him:

> True economics never militates against the highest ethical standard, just as all true ethics to be worth its name must at the same time be also good economics. An economics that inculcates Mammon worship, and enables the strong to amass wealth at the expense of the weak, is a false and dismal science. It spells death. True economics, on the other hand, stands for social justice, it promotes the good of all, including the weakest, and is indispensable for a decent life.[30]

- Economics to Gandhi is essentially the science of human welfare. Its goal ought to be *sarvodaya*, the welfare of all. Implicit in the doctrine of *sarvodaya* is the basic presumption of equal dignity of and respect for the life and welfare of every individual.

- The supreme consideration has to be man. A theory that ignores humanity and its needs—material, mental, moral, spiritual—is meaningless.
- Human welfare focusing on man implies the crucial importance of a decentralized social economy. The ideal is a community political economy allowing for a living interaction, mutual access, and voluntary cooperation of all its members.
- The law of *swadeshi* has to be respected. As we saw earlier, *swadeshi* was to Gandhi one of the most basic organizational principles consistent with non-violence.

From the above foundational premises, can be derived what may be called the principles of Gandhian socio-economic thought. It should be kept in mind, however, that they do not stand on their own, independent of time and place. Instead, they always have to be seen in relation to each other, to their foundational premises, and to the culture and society where they are being applied.

The four Gandhian principles are:

(1) *Non-violent Production-Appropriate Technology*: The term appropriate is used to designate the production function that maximizes human needs satisfaction. According to Gandhi no technology should be used which economizes on manual labour, while there are unemployed workers in the community. This clearly flows from his concepts of *sarvodaya, swadeshi,* conscience and trusteeship. Besides appropriate technology should do no harm to the body, mind, or soul, Machinery, according to Gandhi, should not be turned into a craze. Mass production, yes, but in people's own homes;

(ii) *Non-violent Consumption-non-Possession:* Non-possession follows strictly from the principle of non-violence. The less you possess, the less you want, the better you are. And better for what? Not for enjoyment of life, but for enjoyment of personal service to fellow beings; service in which you dedicate yourself, body, soul and mind.

Everybody is entited to the consumption of the basic necessities but the golden rule for the elite and those in power is to refuse to have what millions cannot have and not multiply their wants:

(iii) *Non-violent Distribution-Equality:* Equality meant to Gandhi primarily two things: First, everybody has a basic right to live, i.e., to meet the basic vital needs and live a dignified life in the community with one's fellows. As means to such a goal he strongly denounced charity, the flinging of free meals at people unable to find work, but advocated guaranteed employment for everybody who wants to work. Secondly, equality is absence of exploitation. He endorsed non-exploitative capital labour relations as well as non-exploitation of manual by intellectual labour and, above all, non-exploitation of the countryside by the city;

(iv) *Non-violent Ownership-Trusteeship*: Trusteeship recognizes the right to private property in the means of production as long as it is responsible to the needs of the community. It is *sarvodaya* extended to the firm. Absentee ownership of capital and land, investment and production violating *swadeshi*, excessive salaries, and expense accounts are not consistent with trusteeship. Trusteeship is also consistent with workers' self-management provided they act as trustees;

It should be clear from the above that the core of Gandhi's thought flows from his view of human nature, its needs and goals—material and spiritual. In this sense his principles depend on Vedic thought though adapted to modern conditions. This is especially the case with his concepts of *swadeshi*, non-possession, trusteeship, non-violence, and *sarvodaya*. It was on the basis of the above principles that Gandhi organized the Congress and its mode of functioning.

Gandhi's Politics and Organizational System

Gandhi builtt up the Congress organization as the mode of creating a new political and social culture in the country. On the basis of his theory of man, Gandhi elucidated a well-considered philosophy of politics which reconciled the claims of the individual, the political community and mankind—the three fundamental axes of moral life for his. Every human being is necessarily an individual, a uniquely constituted, self-determining agent coming to terms with himself and the world in his own way and at him own pace. He is the architect and centre of a unique world of relationships which he structures and organizes in his own distinct manner. To take over his life and run it for him is to violate his integrity, destroy his wholeness and perpetrate a most unacceptable from of moral violence.

Gandhi's perspective also enabled him to notice and highlight some of the morally problematic aspects of the modern State. If man's integrity is inviolate, then the domestic use of terror and wars obviously raised disturbing questions. A similar problem arises with respect to the poor, the weak and the underprivileged both in other communities and especially in one's own. They are often caught up in a vicious cycle not of their own making and their degradation is often the product of a social order upheld and protected by the State. As Gandhi argued, the modern State is a highly complex institution. Much of its violence is institutionalized, structured, exported abroad, perpetrated behind the backs of its members and cleverly rationalized. It does not cease to exist simply because one does not see it on the streets; indeed what occurs there may be only a reaction to it. Gandhi rightly remarked that it is morally arbitrary to be exercised about one form of violence but turn a blind eye to the others. All forms of violence, those of the State as well as the rioters on the streets, raise questions of justification. The former cannot be justified in terms of the inherently vague ideas of law and order or public interest, for one needs to ask why the maintenance of order and the public interest requires such violence and whether a social order that can only be preserved by massive violence does not need to be radically reconstituted.

In Gandhi's view a new type or organization based on non-violence and truth was needed to confront the British Empire. For this, as Parikh points out,Gandhi dug deep into Indian culture and evolved a highly evocative mode of vernacular discourse. Vedic sages and seers had argued over the centuries that profound moral and spiritual insights could not be stated but only hinted at, not described but only pointed to, and could only be expressed through myths, symbols, images and intensely concentrated aphorisms which each individual had to decode and interpret according to his ability. The so-called gods and goddesses with their distinctive physical and moral properties, favourite animals and the intricate myths surrounding them were really ways of conveying complex metaphysical and moral doctrines. Gandhi had mastered the indigenous style of symbolic discourse and fully exploited its obvious advantages. It was familiar to his audience, had a deep historical resonance and fitted in with his theory of the unity of head and heart. It also confused and marginalized the foreign rulers and created a private public space in which he could carry on a public conversation with his countrymen in relative privacy. He not only invented and used symbols but became one himself, and his manner of dressing, walking, talking, eating, sleeping, sitting, raising his index finger and choice of sites for his *ashrama* tapped deep historical memories. The symbols were both packed with and went beyond arguments, and both explained situations and stirred people into action. They gave Gandhi's message a power no other form of discourse could have given it.[31]

The Congress as it existed before Gandhi, was an essentially middle and upper middle-class organization functioning with the blessings of the British government and wedded to the method of constitutional pressure and the goal of creating a liberal democratic polity. Some leaders like Lala Lajpat Rai, Tilak, B.C.Pal and others brought in the lower middle classes, introduced the politics of agitation and gave it a distinctivaly indigenous orientation. None of them, however, had the temperament, ability or even the desire to transform the Congress into an effective national organization capable of reaching out to and mobilizing the remotest villages of India. Almost single-handed and within a remarkable short time, Gandhi metamorphized the Congress into a powerful national organization, brought in the peasantry and some sections of the working classes, set up local units, established a clear chain of command stretching right down to the villages, introduced a system of public accountability and secured the necessary funds from his capitalist friends.

Before long the Congress had built up a remarkable structure of authority paralleling and presenting an effective challenge to the established system, and acquired all the visible and invisible features of a State within a State, capable and ready at the appropriate time to replace the colonial State. Its annual sessions took on the character of a 'national parliament' debating and evolving a consensus on the large issues concerning the country as a whole.

Since the radically reorganized and broadly based Congress brought together regions, classes, castes and political groups that had never before met, let alone working together for a common cause, it had to develop a new way of articulating, debating and resolving their differences. Gandhi's contribution in fashioning the new political culture was considerable. The new culture which held the Congress together before and after independence was an ingenious and highly complex construct forged out of the Vedic metaphysics and epistemology, the inescapable constraints imposed by the struggle for independence and Gandhi's own style of leadership.[32]

Following Vedic thought, for Gandhi human existence was characterized by two fundamental features. First, each individual was uniquely constituted and had a right to live by the truth as he saw it. Second, all men were one: what united them was far more important than what divided them and there were no differences that could not be resolved or lived with in the spirit of charity and goodwill. Since both unity and difference, harmony and disagreement, were the necessary features of human existence, Gandhi argued that every human association must fully acknowledge and find ways of reconciling them.

Since man necessarily disagreed and their perceptions of truth were partial, a sympathetic dialogue between them was the only way to reduce their partiality, resolve their differences and arrive at a higher consensual truth. Gandhi translated this doctrine in political terms and concluded that political parties hampered the relaxed flow of ideas and rendered the resoluion of differences impossible. Since they competed for popular support each had a vested interest in defining its identity in opposition to others and emphasizing its distance from them. In order to have a consensual dialogue Gandhi insisted that rather than form themselves into independent and competitive political parties, different social groups and points of view should remain part of a single larger and loosely structured organization.

Gandhi therefore, insisted that the Congress should become, and ensured that it did become, a broad and loose organization permitting a wide variety of beliefs and the utmost freedom of conscience within the framework of shared political goals. Its objectives were pared down to the barest minimum, stated in highly general terms and stayed clear of controversial social and economic issues. Discussions were encouraged and even debates, provided they were expressions of individual 'truths' and not articulated in ideological terms backed by group alliances. It tolerated, even welcomed, disagreement.

The Congress culture had obvious advantages. It fostered not only tolerance of but also respect for opposing points of view. It avoided ideological rigidity and posturing and encouraged political realism. It accommodated different interest groups and presented a united front to the government. It offered them a much needed public space where they could meet, interact, get to know one another and evolve a national consensus. Above all, it facilitated the emergence of a national political language, a great achievement in a vast country where so many different groups had never before met and talked to one another.

The Congress however remained a loose coalition with poor discipline and weak internal unity. The Congress culture reinforced and was in turn reinforced by its weak organization. It smoothed over differences, accommodated but did not argue out and reconcile the conflicting points of view. In Gandhi's as in the Indian epistemology in general, the doctrine of relative truth largely applied to individuals, not groups. Individual differences were therefore accepted as normal, even welcomed, whereas organized group differences were abhorred.

The organization of the Congress being weak, it was able to network with the masses. The vernacular dialogue based on Vedic metaphysics developed by Gandhi helped to turn the struggle for independence into a mass movement which totally paralyzed the British administration. In a manner of speaking, he become a Vedic *rishi* and what he spoke, the people 'heard'—the parallelism to the *shruti* system is obvious. His stress on the Vedic value of sacrifice and suffering enabled him to create a mass force in which people gave up their jobs, burnt their (English) clothes and sacrificed in various other ways. This was something to which the Empire had no answer. As the economic and political costs of administering Indian reached unsustainably high levels, because the India masses withdrew their consent to British rule, the British had no alternative but to quit.

The loose organization set up by Gandhi, it is clear, followed Vedic principles with the stress being on the eternal values of truth and non-violence, on sacrifice, on the dialogue being conducted in terms familiar to Vedic culture, with the process being a decentralized one with each individual following his own way of action as dictated by his conscience. The 'weak' structure of the independence movement conquered the 'strong' British Empire by laying emphasis on human networking (which led to a mass movement) and stress on Vedic culture and values (which coordinated the masses into an effective force).

REFERENCES

1. M.K. *Gandhi, Hind Swaraj* (Ahmedabad: Navjivan, 1948) p. 39.
2. *Ibid.*, p. 40.
3. *Ibid,*. p.52.
4. R. Iyer, *Moral and Political writings of Mahatma Gandhi.* Vol. 1 (Oxforddd: Clarendon Press, 1986) p. 293.
5. Bhikhu Parekh, *Gandhi's Political Philosophy.* (London: Macmillan, 1991), pp. 20-21.
6. *Hind Swaraj*, note 1, p. 37.
7. *The Collected Works of Mahatma Gandhi.* Vol. 32 (Ahmedabad: Navjivan, 1958) p. 219.
8. Parikh, note 5, pp.30-32.
9. J.V. Bondurant, *Conquest of Violence*, (Berkeley: University of California Press, 1965) p.23.
10. M.K. Gandhi, *Non-Violent Resistance (Satyagraha)* (7th Edition) New York: Schocken Books, 1972 p.10.
11. *Ibid.*, pp. 41-42.
12. *Ibid.*, p.161.
13. Bondurant, note 9, p. 25.
14. Mahadev Desai, *The Gospel of Selfless Action or the Gita According to Gandhi* (Ahmedabad: Navjivan Press, 1946) p.145.
15. Bondurant, note 9, p. 29.
16. J.P. Chander, (ed.), *Teachings of Mahatma Gandhi.* (Lahore: The Indian Printing Works, 1945) p. 21.
17. H.T. Mazumdar, *Mahatma Gandhi: Peaceful Revolutionary.* (New York: Charles Scribner and Sons, 1952) p. 41.
18. *Sarvodaya* means the upliftment of all. To Gandhi *sarvodaya* meant *antyodaya*, that is, upliftment of the poorest and most downtrodden sections of society.
19. Gandhi, *Non-Violent Resistance*, note 10, pp. 48-49.
20. *Ibid.*, p. 113.
21. W.S. Nelson, "The tradition of non-violence and its underlying forces", in G. Ramchandran et al., (eds.) *Gandhi: His Relevance for Our Times* (Berkeley: World Without War Council, 1967) p. 17.

22. Quoted in Louis Fisher (ed.), *The Essential Gandhi*, (New York: Vintage Books, 1962).
23. M.K. Gandhi, *The Collected Works of Mahatma Gandhi* (Ahmedabad: Navjivan, 1958), Vol. 32, p. 402.
24. N.K. Bose, *Selections from Gandhi* (Ahmedabad: Navjivan Printing Press, 1948), p. 39.
25. *Ibid.*, p. 72.
26. See chapter on Gandhi in G.R. Madan, *Economic Thinking in India* (Bombay: S. Chand and Co., 1966).
27. A.M. Huq, "Welfare Criteria in Gandhian Economics" *Essays on Gandhian Economics*, Romesh Diwan and Mark Lutz (eds.) (Delhi: Gandhi Peace Foundation, 1985), p. 68.
28. M.K. Gandhi in S. Nayaran (ed.), *The Selected Works of Mahatma Gandhi* (Ahmedabad, Navjivan Publishing House, 1968) Vol. VI, p. 336.
29. Rig Veda, 1. 164.46.
30. Gsndhi quoted in Mark Lutz, "Human Nature in Gandhian Economics" in *Essays in Gandhian Economics*, note 27, p. 39. Much of what follows is based on Lutz's analysis.
31. Bhikku Parkekh, note 5, p. 207.
32. *Ibid.*, pp. 213-15.

8

CONCLUSION

Vedic management makes the individual—his happiness, uniqueness and liberation—the centre of concern and considers the fusing of the various individuals in a group or nation or organization the task of *dharma* or yoga. In the Vedic scheme, therefore, process is what gives the system dynamism and creativity and there is no strem or structures as such.

Vedic management as a normative system is suffused with the values of sacrifice and service. Its way from the Many to the One is by way of affirmation — using things found in the realm of the Many as a means of realizing the One— as well as the ascetic way of denial for those rare souls in whom such a desire arises. The *dharmic* and yogic ways are the processes through whch integration is achieved in the Vedic system.

The interiorization of the Upanishads and the externalization of the Vedas are harmonized by the *Bhagavad Gita* through its system of yoga. The intention is to manage the inner self along with the management of men and materials as a way of fusing the energy of vision, of calm spirituality, with the energy of intense and efficient action as represented by Sri Krishna and Arjuna respectively.

Gandhi has shown how the use of the principles of Vedic management led to an organization and a system that toppled one of the mightiest Empires known in history.

The question that needs to be pondered over, however, is whether the Vedic managerial system is only valid in a specific culture, namely, the Indian, or does it have a wider application?

The above is not an easy question to answer for the simple fact that no attempt to apply it in a different culture has ever been made. In the post-modern era there have been a number of new ideas and management concepts which have evolved and it would be instructive to see the extent to which they parallel, contradict or supplement the normative Vedic system.

One of the new concepts that has emerged is that of a learning organization. According to Peter Senge a learning organization requires personal mastery, building of mental models, shared vision, team learning and using learning as a principle of leverage. The discipline on which such an organization is based is the systems approach in which thinking shifts from a linear cause-effect relationship to interrelationships and where causality is seen in loops and not as linear.[1]

Fifth Generation Management

Another emerging concept is of co-creating through virtual enterprizing, dynamic teaming and knowledge networking. This is based on the realization that while technology is advancing at a rapid pace, organizations are lagging behind causing Tom Peters, the management guru, to remark: "Could it be that we are putting fifth generation technology in second-generation organisations?" The answer, to the problems caused by the new technologies according to Peters, is integration to make organizations more responsive and agile in dealing with the complexity of ever-changing global markets.[2]

Savage also points out that fifth-generation management as a response to the rapid advances made in computer technology, is not concerned with new ways of manipulating subordinates to one's advantage. Instead, it challenges us to rethink the basics: our values, attitudes, and assumptions about leadership, work, and time. It points to an elegantly simple understanding: we need to be in touch with ourselves — our visions, knowledge, thoughts, and feelings — and with one another in new and creatiive ways. And it assumes that the various functions and companies are capable of working in parallel through virtual task-focusing teams. In short, fifth-generation management is a question of leadership. It is not being preoccupied with one's own power, but with how we empower, energize, and enable one another. It presupposes an integrative environment that puts people in touch with one another's best capabilities.[3]

We know that one of the great challenges of our time is the need to organize to create sustainable communities, that is, social and cultural environments in whch we can satisfy our needs without diminishing the chances of future generations. A sustainable community is designed in such a way that its economy, physical structures, and technologies do not interfere with nature's inherent potential to sustain life.

Principle of Ecology

In our attempts to build and nurture sustainable communities we can learn valuable lessons from ecosystems, which are sustainable communities of plants, animals, and micro-organisms. To understand these lessons, we need to learn the basic principles of ecology— the language of nature. We need to become ecologically literate. Being ecologically literate (or "ecoliterate") means understanding the basic principles of organization of ecological communities (ecosystems) and using those principles for creating sustainable human communities.

Interdependence

The first principle of ecology is interdependence. An ecosystem is not just a collection of species but a community, which means that its members all depend on one another. They are all interconnected in a vast network of relationships, the web of life. There are many forms of ecological interdependence, but the most important way in which the members of an ecological community depend on one another is a very existential way — they eat one another.

Understanding ecosystems, then, leads us to understanding relationships. This is a key aspect of the new thinking that we need to understand in ecosystems. The principle of interdependence implies a shift of focus from objects to relationships. A vibrant community is aware of the multiple relationships among its members. Nourishing the community means nourishing these relationships.

Network Patterns

The concept of the "Web of Life" is, of course, an ancient idea, which has been used by poets, philosophers, and mystics throughout the ages to convey their sense of the interwovenness and interdependence of all phenomena. In science, people realized in this century that the network pattern is not only characteristic of ecological communities but of every member of that community. Every organism is a network of organs, of cells, of various components; and every cell is a network of smaller components. So what we have here is networks within networks. Whenever we look at life, we look at networks.

Feedback Loops

Then we can ask: What is a network and what can we say about networks? The first thing we see when we draw a network is that it is nonlinear; it goes in all directions. So, the relationships in a network pattern are nonlinear relationships. In a network, there are cycles and closed loops; and these loops can be feedback loops.

Because we have feedback in networks, because an influence travels around a loop and comes back to us, we can have self-regulation; and not only self-regulation, but self-organization. When there is a network, for instance in a community, the community can regulate itself. It can learn from its mistakes, because the mistakes will travel and come back along these feedback loops.

So, the community can organize itself and can learn. A community has its own intelligence, its own learning capability. In fact, every living community is always a learning community. Development and learning are always part of the very essence of life, because of this network pattern. As soon as we understand that life is networks, we understand that the key characteristic of life is self-organization.

The lesson for human communities here is obvious. We have interdependence, network relationships, feedback loops; we have cyclical flows, and we have many species in a community. When we take all this together, this implies cooperation and partnership. As the various nutrients are passed along through the ecosystem, the relationships we observe are various forms of partnership, of cooperation. In the nineteenth century, the Darwinists and Social Darwinists talked about the competition in nature, a constant fight to survive — "Nature red in tooth and claw." In the twentieth century, ecologists discovered that in the self-organization of ecosystems cooperation is actually much more important than competition. We constantly observe partnerships, linkages, associations; species living inside one another, depending on one another for survival. Partnership is a key characteristic of life.

The principles of ecology mentioned so far — interdependence, network patterns, feedback loops, the cyclical flow of energy and matter, recycling, cooperation, partnership are all different aspects, different perspectives on one and the same phenomenon. This is how ecosystems organize themselves in a sustainable way.

Principles of Survival and Adaptation

There are two further principles that enable ecological communities to survive disturbances, to adapt to changing conditions. One is flexibility. Flexibility manifests itself in the network structure, because this is not a rigid network, it is a fluctuating network. Whenever we have these feedback loops, if there is a deviation, the system brings itself back into balance. And since these disturbances happen all the time, because things in the environment change all the time, the net effect is a continual fluctuation. Everything in an ecosystem fluctuates: the population densities, availability of nutrients, weather patterns — whatever you can observe in an ecosystem fluctuates.

Creativity

To be able to act like an ecosystem, that is, as a network and in a cooperative interdependent manner, management of an organization has to be creative. Creativity implies appropriate novelty. Many argue that the capacity for creative actions seems to be a basic feature of life. This mysterious ability to transform our thoughts and actions to produce unique behaviour is far from understood. Recently scientists have started to take a renewed interest in this important area.

Studies have shown that creativity is about the quality of originality that leads to new ways of seeing and thereafter developing novel ideas. It is a thinking process associated with imagination, insight, invention, innovation, ingenuity, intuition, inspiration and illumination. However, creativity is not just about novelty: for an idea to be truly creative it must also be appropriate and useful. The related term innovation is usually used to describe the process whereby creative ideas are developed into something tangible, like a new product of practice.

As part of their personal aesthetics, creative individuals have a high tolerance for complexity (some researchers call it ambiguity), disorganization, and asymmetry. They often enjoy the challenge of cutting through chaos and struggling toward a resolution and synthesis.

Creativity is concerned with developing new ides, and to do this we need to see the problem from a fresh perspective, which involves escaping from old ideas. De Bono outlines the characteristics of lateral thinking, a term he coined and which has done much to popularize the idea of creative thinking. He spells out how lateral thinking differs from the more common evaluative thinking which he terms vertical thinking. Recognizing that the brain needs to organize information into patterns, he advocated lateral thinking as a means of escaping from set patterns to new perceptions and more productive approaches.[4]

Managers have also to be willing to take risks. Psychologist Frank Farley has identified and studied risk takers and dubbed them Type T personalities because of their thrill seeking altitudes. Creative individuals as well as daredevils and criminals fit this criteria for Type T personalities, who, he says, constantly seek excitement and stimulation — physical thrills, mental thrills, or a mix of both. The mental risk takers are the one's who create in whatever activity they pursue.

Along with risk taking, moreover, comes the acceptance of failure as part of the creative quest and the ability to learn from such failures. Many people believe that creative geniuses come up with ideas instantly, produce only masterpieces, never have any failures, and never take chances because they always know what they're doing. In fact, the truth is otherwise. Mental risk takers by working at the edge of their competence, where the possibility of failure lurks, are more likely to produce creative results. For some, taking risks in uncharted territory is exciting. Others may not relish the risk, but they accept it as part of the way to reach creative goals.[5]

Intuition

Many have stressed on the need for being intuitive in managing complex issues. Writers on the art of management have recognized that practising managers rely heavily on intuition. In general, however, people have a poor grasp of what intuition is. Some see it as the opposite of rationality, others use it as an excuse for capriciousness, and currently some view it as the exclusive property of a particular side of the brain.

According to Isenberg, managers use intuition in at least five distinct ways. First, they intuitively sense when a problem exists. Second, managers rely on intuition to perform well-learned behaviour patterns rapidly. Early on, managerial action needs to be thought through carefully.

Once the manager is 'fluent' at performance, however, and the behaviour is programmed, executives can execute programmes without conscious effort.

Intuition here refers to the smooth automatic performance of learned behaviour sequences. This intuition is not arbitrary or irrational, but is based on years of painstakng practice and hands-on experience that leads to acquiring the appropriate skills. After a while a manager can perform a sequence of activities in a seamless fabric of action and reaction without being aware of any mental effort.

A third function of intuition is to synthesize isolated bits of data and experience into an integrated whole. Synergy which such an activity achieves is in its essence non-rational because it takes you beyond the mere sum of the parts. It is a non-rational, non-logical thinking perspective.

Fourth, some managers use intuition as a check on the results of rational analysis. Most senior executives are familiar with formal decision analytical models and tools, and those that occasionally use such systematic methods for reaching decisions are chary of solutions that these methods suggest if they run counter to their intuitive sense of the correct course of action.

Fifth, managers can use intuition to bypass in-depth analysis and move rapidly to come up with a plausible solution. Used in this way, intuition is an almost instantaneous cognitive process in which a manager recognizes familiar patterns. In much the same way that people can immediately recognize faces that were familiar years ago, administrators have a repertoire of familiar problematic situations matched with the necessary responses.[6]

Increasing attention is also being paid to human beings as prime movers of societal process. The Report of the International Commission on Peace and Food in drawing up perspectives for the next millenium has this to say,

"...the astonishing magnitudes of the achievements of

the present century...(arise) from a process... (which)... expresses itself as scientific, technological, commercial, political, economic, social and cultural development. But its driving force is social and psychological. Its prime mover is human beings. Becoming conscious of the process of society's past achievements is a key to more rapid future progress."[7]

The Report goes on to ask for a two-fold shift of our attention and emphasis from solving problems to tapping opportunities and seeking to achieving our maximum potential. The world possesses the technology, resources and organizational abilities needed to eradicate poverty from the globe. The reason why poverty is not being eradicated is not lack of material resources. In too many cases the positing of material constraints has become a justification for non-action. The true constraints are not material, the Report points out, but psychological and social; human being are our most creative, productive and precious resource. Human capacity increases the more it is drawn upon. It can never be exhausted. Developing the human resource, thus, should be the centrepiece of all development strategy.[8]

The Report points out the need for a holistic approach which takes into account all the interrelated factors — political, economic, technological, social and environmental — rather than relying on partial strategies. Partial remedies, however welcome or desirable, can always generate side-effects.

Besides all individual achievement is based on prior social accomplishment. The courageous pioneers and talented individuals who achieve more for themselves always draw upon a rich social legacy and build on the ideas, knowledge, discoveries, inventions and innovations of countless people and societies who have come before. Policies should be formulated to reflect the contribution of the collective to all individual achievement.[9]

References from a number of other recent writers on management: Drucker on managing in fast changing times, Peters on how to handle chaos, de Greene on the need for an adaptive organization, and so on could be used in the next, but this is a book on Vedic management and not post-modern management. Therefore quotations from a representative sample of the literature dealing with learning, creativity, networking, intuitiveness, humans as the prime movers in organizations, and so on have been made.

Some of the parallels in the external sense between post-modern management and Vedic management are striking. But so are the differences, especially the internal ones dealing with attitudes and states of mind. Management science, though bringing in pyschological factors into the organisational matrix, is still largely value-free. Vedic management, on the other hand, uses values as the starting point in its delineation of the managerial system. It seems that there is a possibility of synergy between the Vedic and post-modern systems and each individual should be free to work out his own *dharma*, his code of conduct and action.

REFERENCES

1. Peter M. Senge, *The Fifth Discipline: The Learning Organisation* (New York: Duobleday, 1990).
2. Cf. Charles M. Savage, *5th Generation Management* (New York: Business Books, 1991) p. xvi.
3. Charles M. Savage, *ibid.*
4. Edward de Bono, *Lateral Thinking for Management* (Harmondsworth Middlesex: Penguin, 1984) pp. 4-13.
5. Neil Mc Aleer, "The roots of inspiration," *Creative Management*, ed. Jane Henry (London: Sage, 1991) p. 14.
6. Daniel J. Isenberg, "How senior managers think", *Creative Management*, note 5, pp. 48-49.
7. *Uncommon Opportunities: The Report of the International Commission on Peace and Food* (London: Zed Books, 1994) p. 27.
8. *Ibid.*, p. 27.
9. *Ibid.*, pp. 27-28.

Index